The Stress Test Every Business Needs

A Capital Agenda for confidently facing digital disruption, difficult investors, recessions and geopolitical threats

The Stress Test Every Business Needs

A Capital Agenda for confidently facing digital disruption, difficult investors, recessions and geopolitical threats

Jeffrey R. Greene
with
Steve Krouskos
Julie Hood
Harsha Basnayake
William Casey

WILEY

Cover design: Art Director Santiago Eli Lastra, Hogarth Worldwide

EYG no. 010118-18Gbl
ED None

Published by John Wiley & Sons, Inc., Hoboken, New Jersey.
Published simultaneously in Canada.

For general information on our other products and services or for technical support, please contact our Customer Care Department within the United States at (800) 762-2974, outside the United States at (317) 572-3993 or fax (317) 572-4002.

Wiley publishes in a variety of print and electronic formats and by print-on-demand. Some material included with standard print versions of this book may not be included in e-books or in print-on-demand. For more information about Wiley products, visit www.wiley.com.

Library of Congress Cataloging-in-Publication Data

Names: Greene, Jeffrey R., author. | Krouskos, Steve, author. | Hood, Julie, author. | Basnayake, Harsha, author. | Casey, William, author.
Title: The stress test every business needs : a capital agenda for confidently facing digital disruption, difficult investors, recessions and geopolitical threats / Jeffrey R. Greene, Steve Krouskos, Julie Hood, Harsha Basnayake, William Casey.
Description: First Edition. | Hoboken : Wiley, 2018. | Includes index. |
Identifiers: LCCN 2018020487 (print) | LCCN 2018033008 (ebook) | ISBN 9781119417965 (Adobe PDF) | ISBN 9781119418139 (ePub) | ISBN 9781119417941 (hardback)
Subjects: LCSH: Management. | Strategic planning. | Leadership. | BISAC: BUSINESS & ECONOMICS / Management. | BUSINESS & ECONOMICS / General. | BUSINESS & ECONOMICS / Leadership.
Classification: LCC HD31 (ebook) | LCC HD31 .G746 2018 (print) | DDC 658.4/0352—dc23
LC record available at https://lccn.loc.gov/2018020487

V10002764_072618

Acknowledgments

This book represents many decades of creative work by thousands of our EY Transaction Advisory Services colleagues around the world. We are particularly grateful to all the contributors who invested the time, energy, and insight to craft their chapters.

The opportunities and challenges our clients provide us every day are essential to our thinking. Regular discussions with members of EY's Corporate Development Leadership Networks in the United States, Europe, and Asia-Pacific region have inspired many of the themes we share in the following pages.

The project team deserves special thanks, beginning with Jonathan Rozek, who brought invaluable writing and editorial guidance. In addition to being the author of his own chapters, Daniel Burkly played the roles of muse and devil's advocate throughout. Linda Cunningham's project management helped get the manuscript over the finish line. Gaeron McClure led EY's rigorous internal review process, and the book is materially better because of him. Scott Chapski, Mateusz Kowalik, Abin Tijo, and Aparna Mitra supplied their much-needed copyediting, legal, and graphic knowledge. The global Brand, Marketing, and Communications team of Antony Jones, Nicola Gates, and Brielle Roldan sustained this effort from inception.

Intellectual challenges from John Celentano and Anne Board elevated our thinking. Dawn Quinn was present at the creation; it's unlikely we would have begun the book without her enthusiasm. We very much appreciate Richard Narramore, Senior Editor for Business

Publications at John Wiley & Sons, for his substantial advice and patience throughout the writing process.

Finally, and most importantly, we thank our families—Teri Greene, Kamela Krouskos, the Hoods, Shanil and Shamin Lee Basnayake, and Amy Casey—for encouraging us, supporting our work, and helping us grow.

Jeffrey R. Greene, New York City
Steve Krouskos, London
Julie Hood, London
Harsha Basnayake, Singapore
William Casey, New York City

Contents

1

How resilient is your Capital Agenda?

Jeffrey R. Greene

Framing decisions within the Capital Agenda

The Capital Agenda is a comprehensive approach companies should use to manage capital, execute transactions, and apply practical corporate finance tools to strategic and operational decisions. This book synthesizes what we've learned over literally thousands of engagements helping clients as they navigated out of crises to confront technological disruption, unrelenting investor scrutiny, slow gross domestic product (GDP) growth, and geopolitical volatility.[1] EY's Capital Agenda framework has been such a valuable tool that we've built Transaction Advisory Services around it, using it to set priorities for recruiting and talent management, innovation, and thought leadership.

Having a static Capital Agenda, however appropriate for your current environment, is not enough in today's uncertain world. Long-term success comes from building resilience into each element of the Capital Agenda and in the way those elements interact. Banking regulators have mandated well-defined parameters for stress tests of our most important global financial institutions. We believe every *non*financial company should adopt an analogous approach to "future-proofing" its Capital Agenda.

We use a broader, more strategic definition of stress that encompasses not only traditional macroeconomic, sovereign-risk, and commodity-related shocks—such as interest rates, recessions, oil prices, and expropriation—but also forces such as technological disruption, hostile takeovers, and activist shareholders. In this expanded view, companies that make poor strategic decisions or underperform operationally—even in a benign economic and geopolitical climate—can still find themselves facing great stresses. We believe that stress is symmetric; the threat can come from downside risks as well as from missed opportunities.

The Capital Agenda's building blocks

While every company's Capital Agenda is specific to its strategy, operating model, and business environment, Figure 1.1 provides examples of common activities. Each quadrant represents one of the four key processes that make up the Capital Agenda framework:

1. *Raising.* Accessing the capital markets to properly fund growth and day-to-day operations.
2. *Investing.* Deploying capital to new opportunities, both organic and inorganic.

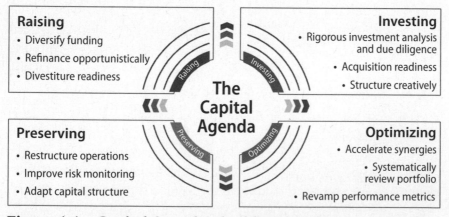

Figure 1.1   Capital Agenda's building blocks

3. *Optimizing*. Reviewing the business portfolio for capability gaps as well as divestment candidates.
4. *Preserving*. Managing risk and adapting to changes in the business environment.

As we'll see, many essential activities affect more than one quadrant. For example, valuation, capital allocation, and tax planning are relevant to the entire Capital Agenda.

Who can benefit from this book?

We created this book to help boards and management teams make better, more informed decisions around their Capital Agenda in an increasingly uncertain business environment that presents both great risks and opportunities every day. How much better? Our friend, Professor Richard Ruback at Harvard Business School, tells students he hopes they'll get 5% better from engaging in his class. It doesn't seem like much, but if you're a professional golfer, 5% better means 14 strokes over four rounds—normally the difference between winning and not making the top 25. In a major tournament, that's likely a difference of more than US$1 million in prize money. As a chief executive officer (CEO) or chief financial officer (CFO), if your stock price is 5% higher each year than it otherwise would have been and that difference accumulates over time, your market value would be more than a quarter larger after five years, and almost two-thirds larger after 10 years—likely enough to ward off a hostile acquirer or activist shareholder. So maybe 5% better at managing your Capital Agenda from reading a book is pretty good.

In these pages we distill more than 400 years of the contributors' collective experience into practical guidance for executives trying to master both the Capital Agenda and the ability to future-proof their companies. We measure business success in two ways:

1. *Shareholder value creation*. How well are you rewarding shareholders, and what's expected over the next two to three years?

2. *Resilience.* Are you adaptable enough to absorb unexpected threats *and* to seize unanticipated opportunities? This applies to evolving long-term trends—like demographics and consumer tastes—and to the rapid pace of short-term changes.

Consistently creating value and maintaining resilience are complicated by the demands of optimizing all the individual elements of the Capital Agenda, as well as managing them holistically. Your ability to control your own corporate destiny faces ever-greater challenges created by:

- Accelerating uncertainty from technology-driven disruption and industry convergence.
- Less bounded macroeconomic and policy uncertainties.
- Growing political divergence with emerging nationalism and subnationalism.
- The formidable power of traditional investment managers and activist hedge funds.

Implementing the Capital Agenda well requires an integrated, strategic focus from C-suite leaders who can see and work across the enterprise. But fluency with the Capital Agenda is necessary for everyone from the board of directors to middle managers. Boards need to exercise their governance responsibilities by asking the right questions that are informed by the Capital Agenda, such as:

- Do our large share repurchases signal to investors that we've exhausted our opportunities to grow organically?
- Is this acquisition candidate a good strategic fit, and do we have the ability to earn an adequate return on our purchase price?
- Are we the best owner of each business in our portfolio?

Leaders in key functions—manufacturing, supply chain, sales and marketing, research and development (R&D)—should understand how their day-to-day activities align with, and support, the Capital Agenda to create value and build resilience. Likewise, practitioners within companies working on strategy, corporate finance, mergers and acquisitions (M&A), tax planning, and operations have essential roles to play in helping make their company's Capital Agenda complete, internally consistent, and resilient. Our thinking should also resonate with advisors looking for new perspectives to address their clients' challenges at the intersection of global capital markets and competitive strategy. Academia represents another important audience: teachers and students who want to explore how financial theory works in practice.

Universal lessons from Allergan and Valeant

The 21st of April 2014 started out like any other beautiful day in Southern California. Despite a Monday packed with meetings, Allergan Inc.'s longtime CEO, David Pyott, took a break around noon to stop by the employee cafeteria and grab lunch.

It was the quiet before the storm.

Within hours, Pyott and his senior team learned of two US Securities and Exchange Commission (SEC) filings that put Allergan in the crosshairs of both an activist shareholder, Pershing Square Capital Management LP, and a hostile acquirer, Valeant Pharmaceuticals International, Inc. The next day Valeant went public with a US$47 billion offer for the Irvine, California–based pharmaceutical company.[2]

Pyott, who had been Allergan's CEO for 16 years, is candid about the takeover attempt. "It felt a little bit like December 1941," he says, and it's not difficult to understand his surprise. Allergan's 2013 revenues had grown nearly 12%, while total shareholder return jumped more than 90%. Few would have labeled Allergan an "underperformer." Its flagship product was growing at double-digit rates, and the company had recently divested a lagging business to free up resources.

It's also not difficult to see how an arbitrageur could develop a rationale for why the company was an enticing target. The year before, Allergan allocated 17% of its total revenue to R&D and 38% to selling, general, and administrative (SG&A) expenses. Both were on the high side for a specialty pharmaceutical company. Given its US headquarters, Allergan also had an effective tax rate 8.5 percentage points higher than the overall average for specialty pharmaceutical and generics players. Moreover, with roughly US$1.6 billion in cash on its balance sheet and little debt, Allergan had a stockpile of financial firepower waiting to be deployed.

These facts created an attractive opportunity for Valeant, a strategic buyer with a lean operating model and a focus on growing through serial acquisition. In his 22 April presentation to investors, Valeant's CEO outlined the "financially compelling" results he believed would come from a merger, including US$2.7 billion in annual cost savings.

But with a market capitalization roughly equivalent to Allergan's and a balance sheet that was already heavily leveraged, Valeant needed help with its bid. Enter Pershing Square, with US$13 billion under management. The hedge fund's sum-of-the-parts valuation analysis showed that its likely return was worth the associated risks of an activist campaign. In other words, as a result of Allergan's relatively high tax rate and operating expense levels, there was a big-enough gap between its market value and its perceived intrinsic value to attract a credible strategic buyer—and a powerful activist shareholder.

A seven-month battle of dueling investor presentations, acrimonious press releases, and litigation ended in a white-knight bid by Actavis PLC valued at more than US$70 billion, roughly twice Allergan's market capitalization before Valeant weighed in. That Valeant ultimately didn't succeed in its bid mattered less to Allergan's stakeholders than the fact that together with Pershing Square it had succeeded in putting the company into play.

Throughout the book we'll consider examples from many industries, but for now there is more for all companies to learn from in seeing how the story played out. Like many corporate tales,

Allergan's journey had a happy ending for shareholders, but a bittersweet one for its CEO and management team. They might be forgiven their *schadenfreude* over what happened to Valeant barely a year later.

Valeant's rise and epic fall

Valeant's stock soared from less than US$20 per share in 2010 to more than US$340 by August 2015, based on a widely celebrated business model of acquiring specialty pharmaceutical companies and individual drugs, then raising prices, cutting R&D spending, and rationalizing SG&A costs. In order to fuel this roll-up machine, acquisitions got larger and more expensive as pharma equities roughly doubled in price. Valeant's debt levels rose to fund these transactions.

In mid-2015, public opinion began to turn decisively against drug companies that were thought to be aggressively raising prices. One analyst published a report saying Valeant had raised prices on more than 50 drugs by an average of 66%—well above the industry average.[3] A congressional subpoena soon followed.

The company also faced investor concerns over some accounting practices and a lack of transparency in dealing with certain third parties. In March 2016, management announced it might be in danger of violating loan covenants. That month the stock fell under US$30 and Valeant joined the "90% club," reminiscent of once high-flying stocks in the dot-com bubble's aftermath. The CEO resigned after seven years at the helm. There were no happy endings for anyone in this story.

To learn from these examples, let's start by examining the resilience of each company's Capital Agenda, because things went quite well for years and then hit a wall owing to unanticipated outside forces. While Allergan's performance looked strong relative to the company's peer group, its *absolute* performance created an opening for Valeant's critique, as some outsiders saw a path to even better results. David Pyott acknowledges that investors might have viewed its high

SG&A-to-revenue ratio as a weakness, but counters that Allergan had "cogent arguments" for its decisions. "We had to create not only sales forces but market competencies," he said.

Two trends converged to create real stress for the company:

1. Investor sentiment shifted in favor of cost reductions to increase margins versus investing in sales and marketing to create longer-term growth.
2. Activist hedge funds attracted more resources and gained credibility with institutional investors.

As the activist campaign wore on, priorities within Allergan did turn from enabling longer-term growth to demonstrating nearer-term earnings. Allergan cut 13% of its workforce and optimized capital allocation. These steps were motivated by conversations with investors, who told Allergan and its board that if the company couldn't get to US$10 earnings per share (EPS), Valeant's offer was too enticing.

Stress test your Capital Agenda

How might management have inoculated itself against these pressures? The well-documented process of scenario planning goes back decades, but we find that very few companies have come close to fully implementing its fundamental practices. One way to get started is to perform a "*pre*mortem"[4] for important decisions. As with many powerful ideas, this one is simple and straightforward to apply to new strategic, operational, and capital decisions, as well as to initiatives already underway. Instead of asking what could go wrong, the team begins by assuming the effort failed in dramatic fashion. Then everyone writes down individually all the possible reasons he or she can think of for the failure, before each is considered in turn for ways to better future-proof the project. Even Nobel laureate Daniel Kahneman, widely regarded as one of the godfathers of modern-day behavioral economics, has complimented the power of the premortem approach.

Here are a few plausible action items that could have come out of an Allergan premortem on its Capital Agenda:

- Strengthen our dialogue with investors to make sure they understand and buy into how our sales and marketing programs will drive future growth.
- Demonstrate the productivity of our long-term R&D investments with compelling analysis.
- Take a fresh look at all costs, and eliminate any unnecessary expenses.

Some of these may seem to use too much hindsight, but they amount to basic tenets about "thinking like an activist" and staying in touch with major shareholders—concepts that all boards and management teams should adopt, and which we discuss in detail in Chapter 13. In 2017, shortly after the US$130 billion DowDuPont merger closed, no less than four activists were criticizing the planned separation of the combined group into three publicly traded entities. DowDuPont responded by surveying its top 25 shareholders before making meaningful changes to its separation plans.[5]

Had Valeant management done a premortem around its business model, it might have given itself some to-dos as well:

- Be transparent to investors about the role that product price increases will play in our ability to extract value from acquisitions.
- Reduce our dependence on debt, in order to build more flexibility into our capital structure in case cash flow falls below our base-case expectations.

Hindsight again? Not really. Though there was additional complexity in the Valeant story, a common trait of roll-up strategies is that they eventually run out of fuel. Often competition bids up the price of desirable acquisition candidates, or the value of the strategic premise erodes—both of which happened here.

Turning to the components of Allergan's and Valeant's Capital Agendas and their internal alignment, we can see strengths and weaknesses:

- Allergan's conservative leverage provided a financial cushion but also suboptimized capital costs, and created the opportunity for a hostile acquirer to tap into its unused debt capacity.
- David Pyott also admits the company should have looked harder at M&A opportunities: "In hindsight, we should have used the balance sheet more aggressively. We were trying to be disciplined," he says. Indeed, had Allergan used some of its balance sheet to acquire a competitor—a move it attempted once the hostile bid became public—it might have moved out of Valeant's reach.
- In many ways, Valeant's capital structure and M&A challenges were the opposite of Allergan's. As debt levels rose for each successive acquisition, capturing the cash flow synergies of increasingly expensive targets became essential to reducing leverage. The cycle ended when substantial drug price increases became untenable.

Premortem stress testing generates valuable insights

Figure 1.2 shows some additional possibilities for answers to the question "What went wrong?" in a Capital Agenda premortem exercise. Of course, many are discovered after the fact—during the *post* mortem. You can use these examples to stress test your Capital Agenda as you build and refine it.

During an introductory meeting on improving transaction processes, an executive said to us, "We have a great process in place to capture lessons learned from our strategic investments. The problem is that they're always the same lessons!" Employing the premortem approach will increase your chances of designing and implementing your Capital Agenda properly in the first place.

What went wrong?	What caused it?
We overpaid for the acquisition.	▪ Our CEO fell in love with it. ▪ Our due diligence did not properly vet the optimistic projections.
We failed to capture the planned synergies for the acquisition.	▪ Integration planning wasn't considered during due diligence. ▪ We didn't allocate enough resources to the functional work streams.
We waited too long to divest an underperforming business.	▪ We thought we could fix it. ▪ The group leader was incentivized on revenue and EPS contributions, not on shareholder value.
We had to retreat from an important market.	▪ A new competitor from another sector provided our best customers with a dramatically better value proposition.
We had to give the activist shareholder a board seat.	▪ We couldn't refute the activist's detailed critiques of our business units' returns on invested capital (ROICs). ▪ We couldn't articulate why our strategy was better for shareholders.
Our stock was downgraded.	▪ We have too much cash unnecessarily tied up in working capital.
We lost money on the joint venture.	▪ The business unit sponsor rotated into a job in another part of the company.

Figure 1.2 Possible answers to "What went wrong?"

Making the most of your Capital Agenda

Keeping in mind the following guiding principles will help provide order and prioritization as you hone all the moving parts of your company's unique Capital Agenda.

- *Principle 1: Enterprise-wide capital allocation.* Investing experts from Warren Buffett to large money managers to hedge fund icons agree that capital allocation is one of the most important functions of your executive team. All types of investment decisions—capital expenditures, R&D, acquisitions, dividends, and share repurchases—must be evaluated using consistent criteria. This applies equally to new uses of capital and to decisions on how to manage your existing business portfolio that represents capital already invested. See Chapters 3 and 4.
- *Principle 2: Comprehensive transaction strategy and processes.* There are well-defined, repeatable practices that raise the odds of success for M&A, divestments, and other inorganic investments. Chief among them is having a clear, actionable view on how you will create strategic and financial value. Another is to build organizational readiness at a tactical level to acquire and divest when opportunities arise unexpectedly. See Chapters 5 and 6.
- *Principle 3: Adaptive financing and payout policies.* Overall capital structure and financing choices for individual investments go a long way to determining your company's resilience. See Chapter 7. Dividends and share repurchases must balance shareholder preferences, operating needs, and risk. For private firms, the decisions concerning if and when to go public can have existential consequences.
- *Principle 4: Finance in sync with, and enabling, strategy and operations.* Your strategy and your operating model are translated into shareholder value through the Capital Agenda. As uncertainty rises, success requires closer collaboration among the policymaking

and implementation teams in finance, operations, and strategy. See Chapter 10. Proper stress testing across the Capital Agenda will help management more clearly understand and better communicate the explicit trade-offs between flexibility and efficiency.

Three essential traits of a sound Capital Agenda

The right Capital Agenda for your business has three important characteristics:

1. *Complete.* In addition to having all the requisite elements, each needs to work properly on its own. For example, a well-functioning portfolio management process helps ensure that every business unit is regularly reviewed using a consistent set of strategic and financial criteria. We cover this in more detail in Chapter 4.
2. *Aligned.* All these elements need to complement each other and align with your strategy and operations. It's no surprise that technology companies whose strategies emphasize heavy innovation tend to be predominantly equity financed in order to cushion the cash flow fluctuations that come with the ups and downs of R&D and commercial execution. Alignment among individual elements also helps executives make trade-offs, such as balancing share repurchases, capital expenditures, and M&A investments.
3. *Resilient.* This is where stress testing is particularly important. A complete Capital Agenda with good alignment also has to help your company thrive by absorbing downsides and, equally important, by taking advantage of new opportunities that crop up. Building divestiture readiness—via execution capabilities, a robust watch list, and virtual carve-out analyses—provides the flexibility to respond quickly both to unexpected cash shortages and to overheated market conditions for in-demand assets.

Performance improvement opportunities

Throughout the book we highlight valuable by-products that come from great execution around your Capital Agenda. These performance improvement opportunities often show up in financial results and operating processes. Though not a comprehensive list, we summarize a few here so you can be on the lookout for them:

- During acquisition integration, learn from the target to transform your own processes (Chapter 5).
- As part of regular portfolio reviews, simulate a *virtual* carve-out of each business. Analyzing the stand-alone costs may shed light on ways shared services can be rationalized (Chapter 4).
- Optimizing working capital management to liberate cash often leads to reduced costs (Chapter 8).
- Performing an activist shareholder vulnerability assessment highlights where information systems need to improve (Chapter 13).
- Analyzing your company's intrinsic value provides the basis for a more compelling dialogue with investors (Chapter 2).

Navigating the book

The remaining chapters first delve into the essential principles and practices for building a resilient Capital Agenda that drives shareholder value (Chapters 2–9). Then we turn to organizational capabilities like getting strategy, finance, and operations to collaborate, and extracting value from outside advisors (Chapters 10 and 11). Next we illustrate holistic applications—real-life examples, if you will—in digitalization, activism, and restructuring (Chapters 12–14). We conclude by outlining a strategic framework to support the Capital Agenda (Chapter 15).

With more than 20 contributors to the book (see Contributor Biographies), each chapter naturally has its own voice, so we hope you'll enjoy the variety as you gain actionable insights to help shape and execute your company's Capital Agenda. If you'd like to explore any of the topics we discuss in more depth, we have a companion website ey.com/capitalagenda that regularly refreshes our current thinking.

Notes

1. Throughout the book the terms *we*, *our*, and *us* refer to the authors and contributors collectively, who in turn represent EY.
2. Jeffrey Greene and Ellen Licking, "Capital Allocation in the Age of Shareholder Activism," *In Vivo: The Business and Medicine Report* 33, no. 5 (May 2015).
3. "What Caused Valeant's Epic 90% Plunge?," Reuters, 20 March 2016.
4. Gary Klein, "Performing a Project Premortem," *Harvard Business Review*, September 2007.
5. David Benoit, "How to Carve Up DowDuPont? Four Activists Sharpen Their Knives," *The Wall Street Journal*, 30 July 2017; "DowDuPont Alters Post-Merger Breakup Plans in Response to Investor Pressure," Reuters, 12 September 2017.

2

Do you know the intrinsic value of your company and how to manage it?

Daniel Burkly

"How are we going to double the value of our business in the next five years?" a business unit leader of a large industrial equipment manufacturer asked her CFO.

The pair had just received this mandate from the CEO, who had watched the company's stock price flounder, and had commissioned a study to determine how to achieve top-decile results for total shareholder return (TSR). The study laid out specific value-creation targets for each part of the company; for this business unit, it was doubling its value in five years. The question was: "How?"

The company had been in extreme cost-cutting mode for several years. Along with doubling the business unit's value, the CEO was asking for more of the same: slash R&D budgets, reduce the sales force, and drive back-office efficiencies.

The business unit leader had two concerns with the push for more cost cutting: first, she had to do significantly more than reduce expenses to double the business unit's value; and second, the cost cutting was becoming unsustainable. The challenge was how to make a convincing case to her CEO. In addition, she also needed to lay out the strategic vision for her own management team.

After putting their heads together for a few weeks, the business unit leader and CFO decided they would need a comprehensive valuation analysis to help chart the path ahead.

The analysis included the following:

- An objective, as-is valuation of the business unit.
- A future-state vision of the business unit five years forward that would represent a doubling in value.
- A portfolio of specific initiatives to close the gap:
  - Organic:
    - Grow sales of existing products in existing markets.
    - Expand into new markets with existing products.
    - Develop and launch new products.
    - Optimize the cost structure of the existing business.
  - Inorganic:
    - Make a transformational acquisition.
    - Complete a series of bolt-on acquisitions the business unit had been strategically focusing on for years.
    - Enter into joint ventures and partnerships to access needed capabilities.
    - Divest low-growth and noncore assets the business unit had held on to for far too long.

This valuation analysis helped answer some key questions:

- How much additional value is there in sustainable cost cutting?
- What is the value of each initiative, given its expected cash flows and risk profile?
- How much value could be generated organically versus through M&A?

- How much capital investment is required to reach the value-creation objective?
- Which project-specific financing structures and third-party investments could enhance value?
- What are the implications for the capital structure of the company overall?

Ultimately, the business unit leader was able to make her case to the CEO that cost cutting was going to take them only so far. Though it was possible to double the value in five years, it would require significant investments in R&D and M&A. She was able to transition to a series of strategic discussions about how to achieve the growth in value through various initiatives that addressed costs, revenues, and capital efficiency. The business unit's rigorous and granular valuation analysis integrated all the levers of value creation, and supported the business unit leader's intuition on the need to move beyond cost cutting.

Closing the gap between intrinsic and market value

For many management teams, meeting or exceeding quarterly earnings targets—and being rewarded with a higher stock price—is the primary everyday focus. Senior executives also carefully track the growth of various financial metrics—earnings before interest, taxes, depreciation, and amortization (EBITDA), revenue, and cash flow—to name a few. One measure that receives markedly less attention from senior executives is intrinsic value.

Intrinsic value represents the fundamental worth of a business based on the present value of its future cash flows at a point in time. Market value is the current value of a company as reflected by the company's stock price. Market value may deviate—sometimes significantly—from intrinsic value. When there is a gap, CEOs and CFOs need to diagnose and act on the reasons: Do investors not understand the company? Or does management lack credibility? Misunderstanding is exacerbated during times of rapid change, such as industry convergence or technological disruption, when investors' perceptions have not caught up with the reality of a company's new business model.

Senior executives overlook a useful management tool when they neglect to link strategic priorities to intrinsic value creation and properly track it at a sub-business level. Activist shareholders often use the size of the gap between intrinsic value and market value to decide whether and how to intervene. Even though your company's market value may be rising, if intrinsic value is a lot higher, the company could be vulnerable. Investors may need to be informed about how the company's strategic initiatives will create value. By communicating this effectively and then consistently delivering financial and operating results over time, senior executives can enhance their credibility with investors.

Before we expand on leading practices, let's review when companies typically perform valuations.

Common valuation applications

Mergers and acquisitions (M&A). Corporate development teams frequently build models to value prospective target companies and help guide the bidding process.

Financial reporting. Tangible and intangible assets, liabilities, and reporting units are frequently valued for financial reporting purposes, typically in connection with a business combination or for impairment testing. Valuations performed in this context must reasonably reflect fair value to ensure that companies' financial statements are reported fairly to investors and to mitigate risk of material misstatement.

Tax reporting. Internal reorganizations normally require legal entity and intellectual property (IP) valuations for tax reporting purposes. These reorganizations result from planning to optimize tax structures and mitigate tax costs. Valuations performed in this context must reasonably reflect fair market value to reduce the risk of scrutiny from tax authorities.

Restructuring. As we discuss in Chapter 14, successful financial restructurings require a well-reasoned valuation of the enterprise and each creditor's claims.

Although companies frequently use valuation in the contexts just discussed, many companies underutilize, inconsistently apply, and even misuse valuation. Most companies can significantly improve the rigor of their valuation analyses and leverage them to make more informed decisions across the Capital Agenda.

Getting more value out of valuation

Generally speaking, most companies underutilize valuation in the essential functions of strategic planning, capital allocation, portfolio management, and investor relations, among others.

Strategic planning

This chapter began with an example of how a business unit leader used a valuation framework to quantify and help structure her strategic options. This is the exception rather than the rule.

Many companies engage in a robust strategic planning process each year that leads to a long-range financial plan. That plan often contains a consolidated earnings estimate. However, rarely do executives extend this process one step further, in order to understand the value of each strategic option. Companies should make it a priority to quantify the effect on intrinsic value rather than primarily rely on qualitative factors. By applying more discipline within a quantitative valuation framework, senior management will be better equipped to make decisions that maximize value creation, as was the case for the business unit leader and her CEO.

As another example, a medical device manufacturer was interested in developing a new line of equipment. The CEO wanted to proceed quickly with a specific acquisition, but the company had two alternatives to an outright purchase: develop its own intellectual property or license IP from a third party for use in certain markets. The CEO's executive team pushed him to slow the process down to allow for a comprehensive analysis to be performed. Though the first alternative (to build) had been vetted and was deemed far too costly from a time-to-market perspective, the second alternative (to license) had not been analyzed at all. The corporate development team concluded that the licensing alternative would create the most value for the company—by a wide margin—while still meeting the company's strategic objectives. The company changed course, deciding to license rather than buy or internally develop the intellectual property.

Capital allocation

Disciplined valuation analysis should be central to the capital allocation decision-making process because it enables management to quantify the relative value creation of various uses of capital, as we discuss in Chapter 3.

Portfolio management

Like private equity (PE) owners, corporations should regularly value each business in their portfolios. Building valuation into the portfolio management process drives visibility and alignment around where and how value is being created and destroyed. Importantly, it also encourages a more proactive mindset. We discuss portfolio management in greater detail in Chapter 4.

Investor relations

With the rise of activist investors in recent years, it has never been more important for companies to align with shareholders on their strategy for creating value (see Chapter 13). Management teams need to create intrinsic value and then make sure investors understand and translate that into market value.

Just as the business unit leader described at the beginning of the chapter used valuation to achieve goal alignment with her CEO, it is possible for executives to increase transparency and buy-in with investors. This could be accomplished by explaining their views on what determines the intrinsic value of the company, including the value they expect to create through various strategic initiatives and operational improvements. Although senior executives shouldn't communicate specific valuation figures directly to public investors, they can use perspectives and insights developed from their own valuation analyses to guide their discussions.

For several years, Pfizer considered splitting into two publicly traded companies to separate its low-growth generics from its patent-protected products. Pfizer's executives were transparent with the board and with investors, frequently discussing the merits and costs of pursuing this strategic option. The analytical support behind the company's communication with stakeholders was an objective sum-of-the-parts (SOTP) valuation that estimated the stand-alone value of each business if it were sold to a third party or spun out. For a period of time, the sum of the stand-alone values substantially exceeded the market value for the company as a whole; it was the opportunity to unlock this value that caused Pfizer to continue to monitor the situation.

Ultimately, after a period of high performance by the company, Pfizer announced in September 2016 that it would remain one public company. According to CFO Frank D'Amelio, "Over time, any potential gap between Pfizer's market valuation and an implied SOTP market valuation has closed." Had Pfizer not performed a robust SOTP valuation and been transparent over time, Pfizer executives might not have been able to make as convincing a case to the board and investors for not splitting up.

Inconsistent applications of valuation

Companies frequently apply valuation methodologies and assumptions inconsistently, often because disparate groups within a company don't coordinate well. Here are some examples of how inconsistency causes suboptimal decision making and creates risk.

Competing acquisitions

Two business units within a large conglomerate were pursuing sizable acquisitions. Both had corporate development personnel who reported to the leaders of the respective units. Both acquisitions appeared to be highly synergistic. However, one of the business unit leaders was far more cautious when it came to revenue synergy expectations; this leader wanted to exclude them entirely from his business plan for the target and, by extension, from the economics in the deal model. The other business unit leader included aggressive revenue synergies. As a result of this inconsistent approach, the transaction that included revenue synergies appeared to create far more value. In the end, the board approved the transaction with the revenue synergies reflected in the deal model and did not approve the other transaction. Whether to include revenue synergies is a legitimate area for debate; however, the company should have ensured that all business units were treating this critical forecast assumption consistently so the board could evaluate investment options on a level playing field.

Tax reporting

In connection with an acquisition, a chemical company engaged a third party, with whom the company had rarely worked previously, to value the target's intellectual property for both financial and tax reporting purposes. The team performing the valuation was not aware that the acquirer held comparable IP, which it licensed internally and externally at an agreed-upon, arm's-length royalty rate. The valuation team did not ask the necessary questions or interview the company's transfer pricing professionals to establish the key facts relating to the IP. Consequently, the third party's valuation deviated from the company's well-established licensing agreements and transfer pricing, which created the risk of future challenges from a tax authority.

Eight ways to minimize misuse and maximize effectiveness

Senior executives have ample opportunities to make valuation a more effective corporate tool. While it's not always easy to embed valuation throughout your corporate decision-making, smart companies are now using it to their advantage. Following these eight recommendations will help you up your game.

1. Optimize the role of senior management

Senior management should provide executive sponsorship for uniformly applying valuation as an analytical tool by:

- Allocating sufficient resources to the development of valuation expertise.
- Requiring that valuation be a component of strategic decision-making processes.
- Relating past results and future plans to intrinsic value in discussions with both internal and external stakeholders.
- Installing a postmortem review process to identify issues and improve future valuations.

Although many tough decisions boil down to numbers—allocating R&D investment, pricing an acquisition, repurchasing shares—leaders should appreciate both the art and the science of valuation. Senior managers need not become number crunchers. However, they must invest the appropriate amount of time to understand what is behind the numbers, in order to balance judgment with financial models.

2. Establish a center of excellence while encouraging collaboration

To successfully perform a valuation, the roles and responsibilities of various functions and individuals need to be clearly defined—and the earlier the better. Those responsible for reviewing analyses should represent a core, centralized team with requisite technical skills, whether from within the organization or engaged externally.

The valuation of a business unit, internal project, or acquisition target is typically a highly cross-functional exercise, requiring data, insight, and expertise from several internal groups, including:

- Financial planning and analysis, for historical data and detailed forecast information.
- Treasury, for input on the cost of capital.
- Operations, to assess the operational risks inherent in the forecast.
- Tax, for effective tax rates, structuring considerations, etc.
- Accounting, for insights on the financial statements.

Relevant information and feedback must flow freely among these groups as the analysis is built and iterated. Achieving the necessary real-time communication can be difficult in a complex global organization, particularly when key players have multiple responsibilities and valuation is not their day job. Executive sponsorship greatly helps to ensure their responsiveness and support, and with keeping the project focused and moving forward.

3. Demand objectivity and intellectual honesty

Many deals, particularly transformatonal ones, are negotiated by the highest levels of organizations. It's common for the acquiring and target company CEOs to agree on a deal in principle and then rely on their staffs to work out the particulars and execute. A significant element of that effort is often a valuation model that calculates the deal metrics (e.g. internal rate of return (IRR), net present value (NPV)). This analysis is usually presented in summary form to senior management and the board as part of the capital-budgeting and transaction-approval processes. What often happens in practice is that companies stretch certain assumptions in order to make the deal economics appealing, or at least palatable, to those in the chain of approval.

Warren Buffett articulated this, as only he can, in his February 2018 annual letter to shareholders:[1]

> *Once a CEO hungers for a deal, he or she will never lack for forecasts that justify the purchase. Subordinates will be cheering, envisioning enlarged domains and the compensation levels that typically increase with corporate size. If the historical performance of the target falls short of validating its acquisition, large "synergies" will be forecast. Spreadsheets never disappoint.*

When two industrial company CEOs agreed to merge, they worked out terms over a private dinner. That initial agreement set off a flurry of activity, including a lengthy regulatory approval process. Both organizations were heavily invested in getting the deal done. The corporate development group of the acquirer found that the expected return on the deal was well below the company's required hurdle rate and, in fact, below the company's cost of capital. As it stood, the deal would be difficult to sell to stakeholders, including the company's board. What ensued was a search under every rock for cost and revenue synergies that could help boost the internal rate of return. As the target's financial condition worsened over time, the deal model underwent countless iterations, each one with more aggressive synergy assumptions—to the point where it was hard to argue objectively that they were reasonable. The deal eventually was approved, many of the synergies were either not realized or delayed, value was destroyed, and the CEO of the acquiring company ultimately resigned.

Unfortunately, this story is all too common. Even though the pressure may be intense, it is the responsibility of senior management and those responsible for performing the valuation to be objective in their analysis. In this example, objectivity would have saved the company from a disastrous acquisition, shareholders from substantial losses, and the CEO from losing his job.

4. Revisit key assumptions frequently

Companies should routinely reevaluate key valuation assumptions to keep pace with changing market dynamics. One example is the hurdle rate that companies use when considering investments like M&A.

Following the 2008 financial crisis, as the US Federal Reserve pushed interest rates close to zero, the cost of capital declined. According to a survey of senior financial executives by Duke University and *CFO Magazine*, almost a decade later many companies had not decreased their hurdle rates in line with the decrease in their cost of capital. The study found that executives were highly optimistic about the economy, but were investing far less than they had in the past, in part because the return on many projects did not exceed their inflated hurdle rates.[2] As markets change and companies evolve, it is important to have a regular cadence for reevaluating and modifying valuation assumptions.

5. Stress test assumptions

Because there are so many subjective inputs, valuation naturally lends itself to stress testing and scenario analysis. However, many companies' valuation models have limited flexibility. There is often just one base case set of projections, and even if other cases exist, they are often quickly disregarded.

A diversified industrial company had long been searching for top-line growth. Amid an energy boom, the company set its sights on targets in the energy sector. When the acquirer was performing its valuation analysis of a target, the financial projections assumed the status quo for the energy industry and the broader economy. Unfortunately for the company, its senior management did not fully appreciate the highly cyclical nature of the energy industry. The deal model included a downside case, but this scenario reflected only modest revenue declines. Almost immediately after the company closed on the transaction, the bottom fell out of the energy market.

The effect on the target's results was far worse than any downside case the company had considered. In retrospect, there had been signs that the industry was on a downward trajectory: energy insiders had already started making moves such as shelving large expansion projects, suggesting they were anticipating a decline. Had the company stress tested its assumptions—and perhaps performed the type of premortem analysis described in Chapter 1—management might have more carefully considered the potential for an energy downturn. It was a reasonable possibility, given energy price volatility. The company could have at least had a healthy debate internally about whether the bid it was considering was too high.

6. Employ analytics

Analytics involves applying sophisticated algorithms to traditional and nontraditional data to identify patterns, predict behavior, and help to make more informed decisions. Analytics enhances valuation in two key ways:

1. Using data visualization tools dramatically improves the clarity with which key value drivers and results are presented and understood.
2. Bringing together disparate sources of information—both structured and unstructured—provides a more complete picture of the future prospects, and more accurately assesses the value of a business.

When it comes to vetting projections provided by an acquisition candidate, analytics can improve both efficiency and effectiveness. Acquiring companies typically impose some of their own views— and skepticism—to scale back the target's stand-alone projections before considering synergies. For both of these steps—assessing management's forecasts and developing synergies—analytics can greatly enhance the simplified approaches that most companies have historically taken, by leveraging large data sets and drawing more informed insights from them.

When a consumer products company considered acquiring a business with a popular niche product in a children's healthy snack category, the target's forecast reflected rapid top-line growth based on historical trends. However, when the due diligence team performed social media analytics to see what parents were saying about the product, the commentary was trending in the wrong direction: children did not like the taste of the snack and were asking for alternatives. Social media analytics provided the insight necessary for the company to reconsider its options. Ultimately, the acquirer significantly reduced the growth expectations and its valuation for the target, and made plans to reformulate the product to improve its taste while taking advantage of the organic brand positioning that the target had created.

7. Perform valuation analysis at a granular level

Valuing your business at a sufficiently detailed level—for example, by product and geographic area—enables you to pinpoint where value is being created and destroyed over time. Management can then make more informed decisions about what to fix, as well as where to invest or divest. This requires information systems to make reliable data available.

One benefit of a granular valuation analysis is that it forces management to objectively assess the risk profile specific to each business. By way of example, a multinational corporation had grown very rapidly through a series of global acquisitions over several years. The company historically used the same hurdle rate on all projects regardless of the unique risks, including geographic area. When the company experienced a series of negative results in certain markets—currency devaluations, regulatory changes, tax increases—it reassessed its methodology for valuing existing and potential investments. It developed a system to consider country-specific risks in markets outside the United States when deriving a discount rate for each investment. By considering the risk-return profile at such a granular level, the company was able to make better, more informed capital-allocation decisions. In addition, by analyzing the appropriate financing for each new investment and current business, managers could build a more accurate bottom-up perspective of the optimal capital structure for their enterprise.

8. Consider alternative valuation methods

When structuring investments, management teams often have options to expand, delay, or abandon projects once they are underway. These embedded options are usually referred to as real options. Traditional valuation methods such as discounted cash flow (DCF) or market multiples struggle to adequately reflect the initial value of such projects and to properly guide decision making around whether and when to exercise each option.

One common way to evaluate real options is by using decision-tree analysis, which provides a framework for considering a broad range of possible future outcomes, and then quantifies an optimal path forward at each decision point. Each option is explicitly modeled within the decision tree, requiring inputs such as the estimated value from exercising the option (e.g. salvage value from abandoning a project) and the risk associated with those outcomes occurring (e.g. discount rate to present value cash flows from a successful product launch).

Real options can arise in capital-intensive industries in which a properly scaled manufacturing plant requires very large up-front investment and several years to build. Managers base their decision to build *today* on forecasts of long-term customer demand and production costs. What if enough demand doesn't materialize? In hindsight, executives will wish they had built a smaller plant. Using decision tree analysis, managers can evaluate the alternative of building a smaller, subscale plant now, waiting a few years to see how demand turns out, and then—if it is strong—building a second plant. Conceptually, the benefit of building the small factory now is the ability to avoid the downside of too-low demand for the big plant. Real options analysis helps quantify this and trade it off against higher operating costs from being subscale, and lost profits if demand is far higher than the smaller plant can supply.

Cultivating a valuation mindset

Thinking about and analyzing the valuation implications of important decisions enables companies to frame opportunities and challenges much more clearly and with a wider field of vision. Valuation can also be used as the common language and framework to enhance collaboration among strategy, finance, and operations, which we discuss in detail in Chapter 10. Having a valuation mindset helps to improve decision making, stakeholder confidence, and performance.

Notes

1. Warren E. Buffett, "Chairman's Letter," *Berkshire Hathaway Inc. 2017 Annual Report*, p. 4 (24 February 2018). http://www.berkshirehathaway.com/letters/2017/ltr.pdf
2. "Getting Over Hurdle Rates," *CFO Magazine*, 12 September 2017.

3 | Are you allocating capital across the enterprise to reduce C-suite stress?

Jeffrey R. Greene

After joining Pfizer as CFO in September 2007, one of Frank D'Amelio's first priorities was to ensure that the company's capital allocation process supported effective decision making across the enterprise. He and Ian Read, who became CEO in late 2010, have transformed Pfizer into one of the most shareholder-friendly companies in the life sciences industry, as acknowledged by equity analysts. That contrasts with prior years, when the consensus view was less positive.

D'Amelio focuses on both the macro and micro dimensions of prudent capital allocation. On the M&A front, Pfizer has been a serial acquirer, executing a range of transactions from the US$68 billion Wyeth megadeal to the US$17 billion Hospira generics bolt-on to the US$645 million tuck-in of gene therapy developer Bamboo Therapeutics. Pfizer has also been a disciplined divester of noncore businesses like Capsugel and Zoetis. In recent years, R&D spending has averaged close to US$8 billion, while the company has returned more than US$12 billion per year to shareholders in dividends and share repurchases. Pfizer has driven across-the-board improvements in working capital management to free up billions of dollars in cash and reduce its cash conversion cycle. During Ian Read's tenure as CEO, Pfizer's annual total shareholder return (TSR) has averaged approximately 15%, compared with 11% for the NYSE Arca Pharmaceutical Index (through 30 April 2018).

Developing this high level of discipline in allocating capital is one of the best ways to reduce stress for CEOs and CFOs. Misallocating capital, in contrast, can lead to negative analyst commentary, a declining stock price, activist shareholders' critiques, or the arrival of a hostile acquisition offer. That's why CEOs and CFOs proactively highlight their approach to capital allocation in quarterly investor calls and annual reports.

By "capital allocation," we mean the processes, tools, and metrics companies use to decide where and when to invest in:

- Working capital
- Capital expenditures
- Research and development
- Acquisitions
- Debt repayment
- Dividends
- Share repurchases

Equally critical are decisions on where to *dis*invest–which businesses, products, and assets no longer make sense to own.

"What we are really looking for," said Charles Kantor, managing director and senior portfolio manager at Neuberger Berman, "is a demonstrated ability to produce cash flow rates of return on total invested capital that exceed the cost of capital. And what we tend to be impressed by are management teams that can talk in an impressive amount of detail when asked one particular question: How does your company allocate capital?"[1]

Eight leading practices for allocating capital

Although specific leading practices depend on each company and industry, as well as on the macroeconomic and geopolitical environment, world-class capital allocators usually have the following eight practices in common:

1. Focus on a small number of metrics that reflect an outside-in perspective and tie directly to creating shareholder value.
2. Employ consistent evaluation criteria and objective processes for all investment decisions.
3. Establish a "cash culture" that prizes cash flow and does not tolerate unnecessarily tying up capital.
4. Take a zero-based budgeting approach to deploying capital.
5. Practice continuous improvement by examining each investment and implementing lessons learned.
6. Embed stress testing across capital allocation to strengthen resilience.
7. Align capital allocation, strategy, and communications.
8. Maintain information systems that generate granular data.

Following is a more detailed and focused look at each of these eight practices.

1. Focus on the metrics that matter to shareholders

Using the right core measures and targets lays the foundation for effective capital allocation. Investors use them to judge short- and long-term performance:

- *Net present value (NPV)*, calculated via DCF analysis, continues to be the best metric for evaluating new capital investments, and for determining the value of assets in place.
- *ROIC* works well for assessing the performance of existing assets, such as business units, products, and brands. Activist

shareholders strongly favor ROIC in evaluating a company's capital efficiency.

- *Total shareholder return* provides an outside-in look at overall company performance. TSR factors into a growing number of executive compensation plans.

Guided by these three critical financial metrics, you can establish processes and select tools for informed decision making around capital deployment.

Note that we do not include two of the most talked-about performance measures, revenue growth and EPS. Both are easy to observe and explain, but they are only indirectly and imperfectly related to value creation. Pursuing growth for its own sake often destroys value, as when companies overpay for acquisitions. Using roll-up strategies to consolidate fragmented industries can create value, as first movers are initially able to acquire businesses at attractive prices relative to the value that can be extracted. But as time progresses, competition for the most desirable targets shifts more and more of that value to sellers through the purchase price. Doing more acquisitions at uneconomic prices (NPV less than zero) definitely grows revenue and can increase EPS, but actually destroys shareholder value.

Repurchasing shares also raises EPS but does not create value by itself. By virtue of basic arithmetic, buying back shares of stock raises EPS for the remaining shareholders, but their aggregate value stays the same—when the shares are fairly valued.

2. Employ consistent evaluation criteria and objective processes for all investment decisions

As a general rule, you should fund all investment opportunities with a positive NPV. So if an incremental dollar is then invested anywhere across the enterprise, it will yield a return equal to the project's cost of capital. If it doesn't, that could be a symptom of deeper problems. CEOs and CFOs deviate from this rule for a few legitimate reasons:

- *Resource constraints.* Consider a technology firm with a finite number of software engineers to staff its investment projects. The company needs to allocate capital to those projects that will generate the greatest NPV for the talent available. Managers should calculate a "profitability index" by dividing each project's NPV by the number of engineers required, and then fund projects from highest to lowest until the engineer pool is exhausted.[2]
- *Difficulty estimating cash flows.* When managers lack confidence in their ability to forecast results, they could decline projects with an ostensibly positive NPV. The nature of the uncertainty may call for an alternative to DCF such as real options valuation.

These deviations from the rule to fund all positive-NPV projects can have far-reaching negative consequences on value:

- *Rationing capital with self-imposed constraints.* When senior management assumes business leaders who make capital requests are gaming the process by inflating cash flow forecasts, CFOs typically respond by setting hurdle rates substantially higher than the project's cost of capital. This sets in motion a vicious circle: managers inflate their forecasts even more and their leaders trust them even less. Discount rates that are unnecessarily high also destroy value by encouraging managers to seek out overly risky projects in order to clear the excessively high hurdle rates.
- *Applying a single, company-wide hurdle rate.* If you set a single discount rate for all investment opportunities, your firm will underfund projects with a lower required cost of capital, and

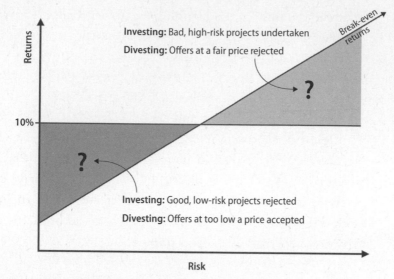

Figure 3.1   Uniform hurdle rate problems
Source: Richard Ruback, Harvard Business School; EY.

overinvest in those with a higher capital cost. Similarly, you may misprice or fail to pursue acquisitions and reject fair offers for businesses that should be divested, as shown in Figure 3.1. We see this behavior when political wrangling over different assigned discount rates overwhelms the CFO, who publishes a single rate, then hopes to subjectively adjust for project-specific risks.

■ *Emphasizing metrics such as EPS or revenue growth instead of NPV.* Some large biopharmaceutical companies that describe themselves as "cash rich and EPS poor" underinvest in value-creating projects in order to achieve earnings targets.

■ *Allowing multiple, inconsistent approaches across the company.* Large, multibusiness firms often use different models, metrics, and processes across R&D, corporate development, and manufacturing. Unless all investments compete for funding on a level playing field, how can you expect to optimally allocate capital?

Or, at the beginning of a planning cycle, firms allocate a pool of capital to each business unit and then end up over- and underinvesting in opportunities across the company.

- *Succumbing to politics, influence, and CEO hubris.* Despite widely reported failures of ego-driven acquisitions, too few companies have sufficient checks and balances in place to ensure a thorough vetting of investment projects. Company leadership needs to encourage challenges from all levels so that the loudest or most powerful voices don't automatically drive capital allocation. Open debate on capital requests that includes multiple perspectives helps test underlying assumptions and drive a merit-based evaluation process.

3. Establish a "cash culture" that prizes cash flow and does not tolerate unnecessarily tying up capital

William Thorndike's study of outperforming CEOs, *The Outsiders*, has become a kind of manifesto for activist shareholders. Thorndike, cofounder of Housatonic Partners, identified the outsider CEO's "genius for simplicity, for cutting through the clutter . . . to focus on cash flow and to forgo the blind pursuit of the Wall Street holy grail of reported earnings."[3] Optimizing free cash flow rather than EPS was the key to a strong long-term valuation. "[T]his emphasis on cash informed all aspects of how [successful outsider CEOs] ran their companies—from the way they paid for acquisitions and managed their balance sheets, to their accounting policies and compensation systems."

In addition to optimizing free cash flow from operations, leading capital allocators are always on the lookout for ways to generate cash from currently invested capital, including:

- *Liberating excess working capital.* In EY's regular industry-specific studies of working capital management, we consistently find that most companies have 5–10% of sales tied up in unproductive working capital. (See Chapter 8 for a full discussion.)

- *Monetizing unused or underused assets.* With greater investor scrutiny of capital allocation, companies have sold more off-strategy brands, excess real estate, and surplus R&D projects; unfortunately, some managers continue to unnecessarily stockpile assets for a rainy day.

- *Divesting businesses that could be worth more to others.* A rigorous portfolio management process regularly tests whether converting a business or holding on to it contributes more to current enterprise value.

4. Take a zero-based budgeting approach to deploying capital

Active reallocation of resource budgets–management time, talent, capital, and operating expenses–can lead to significantly higher TSR.[4] We go further and advise CEOs and CFOs to take a zero-based budgeting approach to *currently deployed* capital. One of our preferred techniques is to perform a "virtual carve-out" of each business unit, regardless of whether management intends to divest it. This involves many of the planning steps for an actual divestment, in particular determining appropriate stand-alone costs in order to value the business properly. With a "what it's worth to us" valuation in hand, management can weigh the likelihood of netting substantially more in proceeds from a sale against the strategic implications and operational feasibility of divesting. We discuss this in more detail in Chapter 4 on portfolio management.

As an added benefit, by highlighting virtual stranded costs–those expenses that would be left behind–the virtual carve-out exercise stimulates an in-depth examination of corporate cost centers to identify rationalization opportunities. In our experience, cost-reduction potential often represents a significant portion of the business's EBITDA.

5. Practice continuous improvement by examining each investment and implementing lessons learned

Installing a robust post-investment review (PIR) process has become axiomatic, yet few companies have adopted the practice. Three main barriers hold management back:

1. Human nature keeps people from admitting their own mistakes, and it's much easier to critique someone else's work. We find the best time for PIR implementation is after a change in senior management, especially the CEO or CFO.
2. The quality of documentation for the initial decision directly correlates with the ability to assess improvement opportunities. If the board-approved financial model, synergy assumptions, and 100-day plan are all clear, then it's relatively easy to evaluate the acquisition after the fact.
3. Once identified, lessons learned need to be put into practice, instead of having to learn the same lessons over and over again. For example, companies can use results from their PIRs to regularly refine their acquisition and divestment playbooks.

6. Embed stress testing across capital allocation to build resilience

Just as stressors come in many forms, companies have multiple ways to improve resilience through their approach to allocating capital:

- *Mindset.* Acknowledge that value creation inherently links to the risks and uncertainties associated with investment evaluation, selection, and structuring. A corporate culture that anticipates and prepares for a wide range of stressors is more likely to thrive.
- *Transparency.* Articulate actionable capital agenda priorities so investors can monitor interim progress and assess management's credibility. In 2016, Larry Fink, chairman and CEO of BlackRock, wrote to all S&P 500 CEOs, "We continue to

urge companies to adopt balanced capital plans, appropriate for their respective industries, that support strategies for long-term growth. We also believe that companies have an obligation to be open and transparent about their growth plans."[5] In his 2018 letter Fink urged CEOs to "publicly articulate your company's strategic framework for long-term value creation."

- *Credibility.* Establish a track record with investors of delivering on your capital plan with strong relative TSR in good times and bad, in order to ward off activist critiques and hostile acquirers. When Bill McNabb was CEO of Vanguard, one of the world's largest investment managers, he counseled:

> *From Vanguard's point of view, we're in the relationship to maximize the value of the longest of long terms for our fund investors. We understand that things don't always go up in a straight line. So if we have a good relationship with a company, they have a great opportunity to tell us their story. If there are performance problems, for example, either own those problems or tell us what you're doing to fix them.*[6]

- *Agility.* Streamline decision making so you can react quickly to new opportunities and threats as they emerge. Complement this agility by maintaining sufficient financial capacity to seize attractive investment opportunities that arise under high uncertainty. For example, empirical evidence supports the wisdom of buying early within a wave of industry consolidation or restructuring. One study found that early acquirers earned returns seven percentage points higher than those who bought near a wave's peak.[7]
- *Natural hedging.* Fund multiple emerging business model experiments to hedge against strategic obsolescence. With the accelerating pace of disruptive forces like digitalization that affect core elements of every value chain, selecting a single strategy that will succeed is not possible.

7. *Align capital allocation, strategy, and communications*

Companies set strategy by deciding in which markets to operate, how to serve customers, and which activities will result in superior shareholder returns. Effective capital allocation translates these choices into economic reality. In the words of Richard Brealey and Stewart Myers, "Strategic planning is a top-down approach to capital budgeting: you choose the businesses you want to be in and make the capital outlays for success."[8] Within your organization, executives need a common understanding of how they'll make capital allocation decisions to implement your strategy. The most important guiding principles are setting investment priorities and defining how they will balance among the following trade-offs (for more information, see ey.com/capitalagenda):

- Organic versus inorganic growth
- Short-term versus long-term results
- Low-risk/low-return versus high-risk/high-return investments
- Reinvestment versus shareholder payouts
- Dividends versus share repurchases

EY recently facilitated a capital allocation workshop for 20 senior executives at a Fortune 50 company. During the debriefing, one of the operations leaders said the session was very valuable "because we learned how the CFO thought about setting investment priorities." Not surprisingly, much of the self-diagnosis during the workshop centered on the lack of consistency in investment criteria across organizational silos.

CEOs and CFOs must also communicate this shared view of value creation to investors, creditors, and other external stakeholders. Two important success criteria are transparency—"Do they understand it?"—and credibility—"Do they believe in it?" Transparency and credibility are essential not only for resilience but also for converting strategy and operations into value. Doug Giordano, Pfizer senior vice president, worldwide development, explains how investor credibility enables management's flexibility:

> *If investors see you as prudent stewards of capital and you're actually beginning to reap some current benefit from past investments, they will give you more of an opportunity to invest for the long term. If you start to lose that credibility, investors are going to want their money back sooner, in the form of dividends and repurchases.*[9]

8. Maintain information systems that generate granular data

Information systems and management accounting policies enable effective capital allocation when they supply data to support decision making around new investments and already deployed capital. With activist shareholders' focus on capital efficiency, your inability to calculate ROIC for individual businesses, products, geographies, and other assets can be a point of vulnerability. Achieving this level of accuracy depends on economically rational cost allocations that remain consistent over time, as well as establishing reliable balance sheets for each business. Management incentives will align better with desired outcomes when business unit profit-and-loss statements (P&Ls) reflect a charge for their use of capital. For performing a virtual carve-out, critical data include each entity's tax attributes and its role in the parent's overall tax strategies (such as transfer pricing).

Evaluating individual investment opportunities: Quantify, debate, judge

As we discussed in Chapter 2, a valuation framework is critical for informed decision-making, and senior executives should invest sufficient time to understand what is behind the numbers. Although DCF provides the core analytical underpinning for decisions, we find that many senior executives and even practitioners are skeptical of relying primarily on DCF. In fact, allocating capital requires balancing the qualitative and quantitative, both art and science. People make bad decisions when the pendulum swings too far toward pure judgment or to just letting the numbers decide. We prefer a simple three-step approach—quantify, debate, judge—which we adapt to each situation (see Figure 3.2):

1. *Quantify.* The two main ingredients for building a DCF model are projecting cash flows and selecting discount rates. The basic techniques for applying the capital asset pricing model (CAPM) are outside the scope of this book, but well documented elsewhere.[10] When reviewing DCF models, senior executives need to ask:

   ○ Do the cash flows represent *expected* results? Ideally, model builders consider a suitable range of future outcomes and objectively probability-adjust them to arrive at expected cash flows.

   ○ Does the discount rate match the investment's systematic risk? Practitioners often give in to the temptation to add a subjective premium to reflect perceived risks that do not belong in the cost of capital.

   ○ How do we adjust for biased cash flows, i.e., when they don't represent expected results? Whether the adjustment is made in the discount rate or in the cash flows themselves has significant implications for the valuation result.[11]

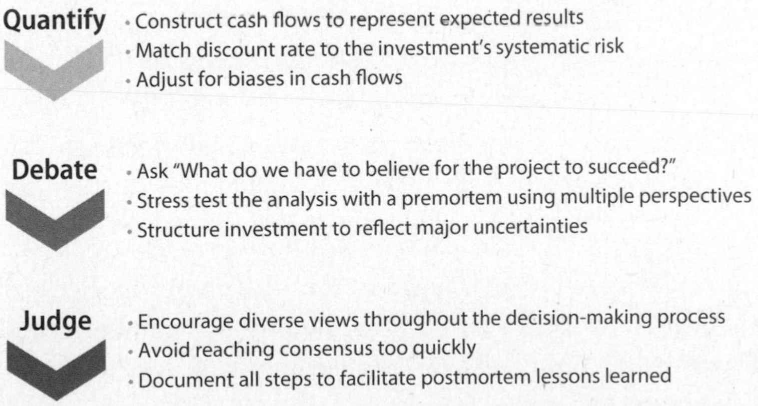

Quantify
- Construct cash flows to represent expected results
- Match discount rate to the investment's systematic risk
- Adjust for biases in cash flows

Debate
- Ask "What do we have to believe for the project to succeed?"
- Stress test the analysis with a premortem using multiple perspectives
- Structure investment to reflect major uncertainties

Judge
- Encourage diverse views throughout the decision-making process
- Avoid reaching consensus too quickly
- Document all steps to facilitate postmortem lessons learned

Figure 3.2 Putting the quantify-debate-judge approach into action

2. *Debate*. Well-structured investment models enable executives to assess not just the assumptions but the causal connections embedded in each model. They need to ask: "What do we have to believe for this project to succeed?" Other important components are:

- Include diverse representation to bring multiple perspectives to bear. For example, major R&D investments will benefit from challenges from both manufacturing and marketing. Though diversity in decision making sounds logical and straightforward, surprisingly few companies do it well. One way to get multiple perspectives is to be explicit that you are seeking (and not just tolerating) substantially different viewpoints–and rewarding those who step up. For real change to happen, this tone has to be set from the top, and over time it has to become part of your culture.

- Stress test the "quantify" analysis by performing a premortem (as we discuss in Chapter 1). Identify major uncertainties and understand possible paths for how they may resolve over time. Use this information to evaluate whether restructuring the investment could provide more flexibility and defer some up-front capital commitments.

3. *Judge*. Once executives have fully vetted the models and numbers, they can make a more informed decision. Be careful not to reach consensus too quickly, before everyone has a chance to be heard and considered, including strategy, finance, and operations stakeholders, as we discuss in Chapter 10. Be conscious of the trade-offs between consensus building and the need to make high-velocity decisions. To facilitate *post*mortem analysis to improve future decisions, document each of these three steps carefully.

You can apply the quantify-debate-judge approach to all capital investment opportunities. In the following section we expand on two particularly tricky ones.

Research and development

Applying our quantify-debate-judge approach to R&D is particularly challenging for pharmaceutical companies because any positive cash flows from new drugs come years after committing substantial R&D funds; quantitative analyses based on DCF are extremely sensitive to underlying assumptions. Pharmaceutical executives might base R&D funding primarily on the judgment calls of senior scientists because of their own discomfort with relying on a "cloud of numbers."

Here are a couple of reasons for a more balanced consideration of quantitative analysis:

- Regardless of the uncertainties around future outcomes from such investments as early-stage oncology drug candidates, oil exploration, or geographic expansion into emerging markets, investors will do their own valuations of these assets when gauging the company's stock price. CEOs and CFOs need to have a well-defined point of view on valuation to guide investor discussions.
- Structuring investments like these—with payoffs far in the future—often requires reaching agreement with multiple third parties over how to share capital contributions, operating expenses, and profits. This can't be done with a qualitative focus; you need a thorough quantitative understanding of the risks, returns, and valuation implications under various structures.

Share repurchases

We agree with Warren Buffett's guidance that, under most circumstances, you should repurchase shares only when both of these two situations exist:

1. *Share price is well below intrinsic value.* The converse, buying back stock when market value is above intrinsic value, transfers value from remaining shareholders to the sellers.

2. *Cash held exceeds operational and liquidity needs.* Assuming the current capital structure is optimal, repurchasing shares when cash is below these levels makes the firm less resilient. Alternatively, CFOs may want to borrow to fund repurchases if the company is underleveraged.

Senior management and boards frequently justify share repurchases to offset the dilutive effects of stock-based compensation. However, stock-based compensation is a very real expense to shareholders: if companies repurchase at a premium to intrinsic value, they exacerbate the negative effects on shareholder value. Boards need to be on the lookout for executives buying back shares with the primary purpose of raising EPS simply by reducing the number of outstanding shares.

So, under what other circumstances does repurchasing shares actually create value? Because stock prices are based on investor expectations about future management decisions, buybacks can increase value by signaling to investors that they should change their views. If shareholders assign a reasonable probability to management's overpaying for acquisitions or overinvesting in unprofitable businesses, then they could view management's diverting more capital to repurchases as value creating. Signaling can work in the other direction, too. If investors infer that management is returning cash because the company lacks worthy investment opportunities, they will likely drive down the share price.

Low interest rates and activist investor pressure have also been major factors in recent repurchases. Empirical data show that companies tend to increase repurchases when their share prices are trading near cyclical highs, when cash tends to be most plentiful. During these times, CFOs have a greater incentive to scrutinize whether repurchasing is a prudent use of capital.

"Capital allocation is a contact sport"

Warren Buffett has always focused on the centrality of capital allocation for Berkshire Hathaway's success. During the 2017 Annual

Shareholders Meeting, he spoke about the challenge his successor would face: "The next manager in the decade is going to have to allocate maybe $400 billion . . . and it's more than has already been put in . . . So you need a very sensible capital allocator in the job of being CEO of Berkshire and we will have one . . . It probably should be very close to their main talent."[12]

During his November 2017 Investor Update, General Electric's new CEO, John Flannery, touched on many of the tenets we've advocated in this chapter, in particular: an enterprise-wide approach, robust analytics, outside-in perspectives, broad-based debate, and post-investment monitoring. "Every single dollar that we're spending and investing is a capital allocation decision . . . and I expect the businesses to be intensely analytical about it . . . This is a deeply rigorous, quantitative, market-based exercise. That's what I expect of the teams. I expect rigorous debate. I expect rigorous tracking of how things are going. I expect a lot of pushback. Capital allocation is a contact sport."[13]

Notes

1. "Enterprise Valuation Roundtable Presented by Ernst & Young," *Journal of Applied Corporate Finance* (Spring 2007).
2. For more discussion, see Richard A. Brealey and Stewart C. Myers, *Principles of Corporate Finance*, 6th ed. (New York: Irwin/McGraw, 2000), 108–110.
3. William N. Thorndike Jr., *The Outsiders: Eight Unconventional CEOs and Their Radically Rational Blueprint for Success* (Boston: Harvard Business School Press, 2012), 9.
4. Yuval Atsmon, "How Nimble Resource Allocation Can Double Your Company's Value," McKinsey & Company, August 2016.
5. Laurence D. Fink, "2016 Corporate Governance Letter to CEOs," BlackRock, 1 February 2016.
6. "Getting to Know You: The Case for Significant Shareholder Engagement," posted by F. William McNabb III, Vanguard, on

the Harvard Law School Forum on Corporate Governance and Financial Regulation, 24 June 2015.

7. Gerry M. McNamara et al., "The Performance Implications of Participating in an Acquisition Wave," *Academy of Management Journal* 51, no. 1 (2008), 113–130.

8. Brealey and Myers, *Principles of Corporate Finance*, 6th ed., p. 1010.

9. Jeff Greene and Andy Brogan, "Getting from There to Here: Stress-Testing Today's Capital Agenda with Tomorrow's Scenarios," *Harvard Business Review Analytics Services*, May 2016.

10. See, for example, Brealey and Myers, *Principles of Corporate Finance*, 6th ed., p. 36.

11. For an excellent practical discussion, see Richard S. Ruback, "Downsides and DCF: Valuing Biased Cash Flow Forecasts," Harvard Business School, *Journal of Applied Corporate Finance* (Spring 2011).

12. Warren Buffett, "Berkshire Hathaway Inc. 2017 Annual Shareholders Meeting transcript", Omaha, NE, May 6, 2017. Available at http://minesafetydisclosures.com/blog/2017/5/29/2017-berkshire-hathaway-shareholders-meeting-transcript

13. John L. Flannery, "General Electric November 2017 Investor Update transcript", Imperial, PA, November 13, 2017. Available at https://www.ge.com/investor-relations/sites/default/files/GE-USQ_Transcript_2017-11-13.pdf

4

Are your portfolio reviews timely, objective, and thorough?

Jeffrey R. Greene and Jeff Wray

In October 2017, Honeywell announced not one but two divestments representing close to US$7.5 billion in revenues. It planned to execute each via a tax-free spin-off and receive total dividends of US$3 billion at closing. For most companies, a single carve-out would be a major undertaking. For Honeywell, these were just two more transactions in a 15-year journey of prolific portfolio reshaping that included close to 100 acquisitions interspersed with 70 divestments.

The most recent moves resulted from a comprehensive portfolio review process that the new CEO, Darius Adamczyk, described as "objective and fact-based, involving extensive analysis and input from industry experts and participants as well as from our shareowners. The foundation of the announcement was a set of criteria ... against which each business was measured."[1] Responding to an analyst's question about future investments, he went on to say, "So the punchline for me is, we're going to be very active in the M&A arena. In terms of prioritization, I think now, given these two spins and given . . . the optimized capital structure, I'm very excited about investing in any of the four [remaining business] platforms."

Even Daniel Loeb, the prominent shareholder activist who had been agitating for a different path, said through a spokeswoman that he was pleased the board and management chose to conduct a thorough portfolio review and agreed that Honeywell should narrow its business focus. He added that he was confident Adamczyk's "commitment to continuous portfolio optimization will further improve shareholder value."[2]

The Honeywell story demonstrates how applying the capital allocation practices we advocated in Chapter 3 drives shareholder value through proactive portfolio management. That's also the clear message we hear from business leaders, investors, and academics, and what we observe in the capital markets. In today's highly uncertain environment, companies cannot afford to be without a well-executed process for deciding which businesses to buy and sell, and when—the essence of portfolio management.

Amid this volatility, CEOs and CFOs should take the offensive in articulating why each business belongs in the portfolio, and lay out clear performance metrics so investors and lenders have sufficient visibility into strategy and operations. When investors understand current and projected ROIC for each business, and see credible plans to improve it, they will be much more willing to support you even when short-term performance lags.

Great uncertainty also puts a premium on a company's ability to react quickly both to unexpected opportunities—acquiring a suddenly weakened competitor, for instance—and to threats such as loss of profitably due to exchange rate shifts. Rigorous portfolio decision making helps maintain sufficient financial capacity by efficiently pruning noncore and chronically underperforming businesses.

Diagnosing the health of your portfolio management process

Portfolio management is about strategy, planning, and processes. To assess the strengths and weaknesses in your current approach, consider the following questions:

1. Clearly articulated strategy
   - How recently have you refreshed your strategy with significant input from external stakeholders?
   - How does each component of your business portfolio complement the enterprise strategy?
   - In response to an unsolicited (hostile) offer or an activist's critique, could you defend the intrinsic value of each business unit and its contribution to the portfolio with previously quantified analysis?
2. Disciplined methodology
   - Do you employ the same investment model and metrics to evaluate existing businesses as you do for new uses of capital, such as M&A, capital expenditures, R&D funding, and market entry?
   - How often do you review your strategic and financial criteria to reflect changes in economic outlook, capital costs, and industry dynamics?
   - Can you calculate the economic ROIC and the appropriate risk-adjusted discount rate for each business?
3. Flexibility to react to market conditions
   - Do you maintain a current watch list and sufficient financial flexibility to outmaneuver competitors if an attractive acquisition becomes available?
   - How quickly could you execute a divestment for full value in response to an internal need for liquidity or high interest from potential buyers?

4. Alignment with internal processes and incentives
   ○ When was the last time you used your planning process to test how enterprise value would be affected by alternative portfolio strategies or external scenarios?
   ○ What metrics does your performance management system use to balance incentives between acquiring and divesting to create shareholder value? Does your corporate culture favor acquiring over divesting?
   ○ Is it clear who in the organization has the mandate to review and make needed changes to the portfolio?

Preparation drives value

For many companies, extensive portfolio management tends to be undertaken in reaction to cash needs or market developments. Yet we know that there is now a whole group of *external* players—analysts, private equity, hedge funds, institutional investors, and the press—who are doing portfolio reviews on your company, whether you want them to or not. We discuss activist shareholders in detail in Chapter 13.

We've observed corporate acquisition skills improving steadily over the past decade, but divestment practices have been slower to evolve. Even companies that execute divestments well tell us they rarely sell the right business at the right time. One corporate development officer we know commented that "some businesses are like ice cubes—the longer you hold them the less they're worth." Both PE and strategic acquirers, of course, expect bargains when buying from sellers who just want to get rid of an underperforming business that has become a distraction to management, a sore point with the board, or a target for negative analyst commentary.

An acquisition perspective

Systematic portfolio management also identifies potential acquisition and alliance needs proactively. Companies with a solid understanding of the gaps in their business portfolio—and sufficient financial capacity—are better able to react quickly when buying opportunities arise. A complementary leading practice: developing a watch list of desirable acquisition targets and building relationships that bring early indications of when they may become available.

Michael Porter has commented on the benefits of anticipating favorable industry evolution: "[C]reative strategists may be able to spot an industry with a good future before this good future is reflected in the price of acquisition candidates."[3] Applying this observation to divestments, we suggest that forward-thinking management teams should try to anticipate unfavorable industry developments before they are reflected in the value of existing portfolio businesses.

Approach ownership flexibly

The value creation methods of PE firms have long been held out to public companies as a role model for generating above-market returns. Their approach includes a single-minded focus on cash flow and financial metrics, along with a willingness to sell at any time for the right price. Corporate managers should have the mindset of "flexible ownership" for their businesses—a hybrid approach between PE's "buy-to-sell" model and the traditional "buy-to-keep" model of public companies.[4] Three skills are critical to successfully implementing the flexible ownership strategy:

1. Correctly identifying and valuing businesses with improvement potential
2. Turning around poorly performing businesses
3. Managing a steady stream of acquisitions and divestments

Shareholders benefit most when companies take a proactive approach and systematically evaluate the hold/fix/sell question for each of their businesses.

Implement world-class portfolio management

Turning portfolio management into a core competency requires a corporate commitment to align incentives, structure, processes, and tools. Getting all of this right helps lead to well-timed divestments, stronger balance sheets, and increased readiness for opportunistic acquisitions—all very big pluses in the current economy.

Articulate your value creation model and supporting metrics

- Corporate and business unit strategy should be translated into well-defined financial criteria for each business unit. Boards and CEOs need to clearly communicate, both internally and externally, the basis for investment decisions. For example, how will managers be asked to trade off revenue growth, earnings per share, and ROIC?
- Management needs to make clear how it balances strategic and financial criteria. Will an unprofitable business be retained because it provides access to an important emerging market? Will a strong financial performer be divested to raise cash and shore up the balance sheet? In leading practice companies, the head of strategy and the corporate development officer work together to address these questions, combining the best strategic insights and analysis with the discipline of corporate finance.

Establish meaningful units of analysis

Though most portfolio management focuses on global business units, there are other useful ways to segment the enterprise. Businesses also can be examined by region. Technology and life sciences firms also consider product lines, platforms, and alliances when evaluating their portfolios. Consumer companies tend to look at a combination of geography and business unit. For example, Nestlé has stayed committed to its confectionery business globally but has decided to divest it in the United States because of the brand footprint and competitive landscape.

Calculate threshold values for each business

PE funds always have in mind current valuations for their portfolio companies, but rarely do corporations objectively value each business. Doing so regularly is a best practice. It forces each unit's leaders to be explicit about how they plan to deliver shareholder value over time, and to develop a point of view on scenarios for how their industry may evolve, particularly given the current economic outlook.

Having up-to-date threshold values allows management to quickly respond to unsolicited acquisition interest in all or part of the company. Without a current valuation in hand, hostile bidders can have a head start in persuading investors that their offer is superior to the status quo.

Employing a common valuation model across the company also helps promote a shared view of value creation. In world-class corporate development groups, standard valuation models are utilized in acquisition processes, but often these models aren't applied to portfolio management. As debt and equity capital costs change, companies should rethink the discount rate assumptions embedded in their DCF calculations, which makes the need for institutionalized valuation methods and processes all the more pressing. We explored these challenges in Chapter 2.

As part of preparing stand-alone valuations, managers should be especially careful to quantify shared costs and benefits among business units and with the parent. Any potential divestment analysis should anticipate negative synergies—such as lower volumes under corporate purchasing agreements—and include a remediation plan for stranded costs.

Scan the external environment

As we've discussed, leading portfolio managers regularly assess the gaps in their business and scan the market for acquisition candidates that could fill those gaps. Conversely, a business that fits well strate-gically and generates healthy returns may be a divestment candidate if someone else is willing to pay more than it's worth to the current owner. It may be one of the few players in an industry segment that has suddenly become very desirable to potential acquirers willing to pay an above-market premium for access. Managers should be on the lookout for buyers that have unique synergies. Keeping track of market valuations for similar public businesses provides a benchmark for your portfolio companies.

The strategy group also needs to be alert to pending industry developments—new entrants, regulatory changes, demographic shifts, and technological breakthroughs—that could put a business unit at a disadvantage. Early warnings allow management to proactively decide whether divesting is the best response.

Build a systematic, objective process

The best analytical tools and high-quality information won't yield the right portfolio moves if decision making is flawed. In designing the process, senior management should allocate clear roles and responsi-bilities to business units and corporate staff. Some companies reserve for corporate staff any divestment decisions, with the business units submitting detailed plans for addressing underperforming businesses.

Another design concern is whether and where to build dedicated resources. In order for portfolio management to be a core competency, some people may need to work on it full-time. This is analogous to the corporate development function embodying the company's core institutional knowledge on M&A execution.

Challenge your "conglomerate rationale"

In the absence of a compelling explanation for how all your busi-nesses fit within the same enterprise and where the corporate parent adds value, the whole will be worth less than the sum of its parts to investors. See Chapter 2. This conglomerate discount is well documented in academic literature. Though there are perfectly good reasons for conglomerates to exist, they are frequently overwhelmed by the costs of maintaining a multibusiness firm.

Thinking through your "conglomerate rationale" requires an honest appraisal of why sometimes disparate businesses belong together, and a readiness to act if pieces no longer fit. Are there operational synergies such as shared plants, technologies, and distribution channels? Does the corporate parent possess unique skills such as personnel development, capital allocation, or performance management that can be leveraged across its portfolio? In emerging economies, conglomerates can sometimes provide access to capital and talent that may be more efficient and effective than relying on external markets locally.

However, there is sufficient empirical and anecdotal evidence to make investors skeptical of a conglomerate premium in most situations. For example, individual businesses often need their own capital structure, tax planning, and shareholder base. Where a business is in its life cycle—start-up, growth, maturity, decline—dictates the kinds of management skills needed. Rarely is the same corporate team able to add optimal value at each stage for each business.

The value-creating effects of divestments, including spin-offs, have been confirmed by numerous academic studies, and increasingly reflected in activists' critiques in recent years:[5]

- Increased management focus on the remaining businesses.
- Better investment decisions, including reduction of cross-subsidies for underperforming businesses.
- Improved transparency for investors.
- Better fit with public investor segments and with potential acquirers.

The more focused a business, the easier it is to align compensation with shareholder value. And in public companies those managers get clearer feedback from the capital markets—an outside-in approach to performance management.

Can "virtual" carve-outs show the way to cost reduction?

"I love stranded costs." That's the way a Fortune 200 CFO put it when implementing a recent divestment. What he meant was that the carve-out transaction highlighted cost-cutting potential in the parent company. A process that strives for accurate cost allocations across a corporate portfolio will naturally challenge the need for certain expenditures and activities.

A well-run carve-out routinely uncovers substantial cost reduction opportunities in the business being divested. In one situation, the annual benefit amounted to more than 25% of the business's reported EBITDA. Management was able to implement some cuts and sufficiently document the others so the final sales price reflected their value to the buyer.

Given such outcomes, should CFOs simulate a carve-out of each business unit as a way to surface possible cost rationalization opportunities? Certainly once a systematic portfolio management process is in place, very little incremental effort would be required to do so. In some cases, however, information systems would need to be revamped to provide adequately detailed cost data. One indication this idea is catching on: the growing number of companies reorganizing so they can report detailed business unit results and provide more transparency to investors.

Confront barriers to success

Why aren't more companies taking a systematic approach to portfolio management? As with many business problems, there are multiple causes, and almost everyone shares some responsibility for suboptimal performance.

Misaligned incentives

Successful managers advance their careers by building and sometimes by turning around businesses. Gaining recognition is usually easier when you run a large group. As long as the primary financial metrics that drive executive compensation and promotion are revenue growth and earnings per share, operating managers will be reluctant to seriously consider selling off portions of their portfolio.

What's more, divesting is often perceived as admitting a mistake. It's rare to see a corporate executive celebrated for a well-executed divestment. And when a sale happens, the group leader does not get to keep the proceeds to reinvest in other businesses. Instead, the funds revert to headquarters' control.

Conflicting interests

The uncomfortable reality is that a solid portfolio management process relies in part on judgment and information from managers and staff whose jobs may be affected negatively by a possible divestment.

Complexity

In contrast to PE-held portfolios, large conglomerates don't have the resources to provide the equivalent of a hands-on, independent board for each business that stays in touch with the environment, closely monitors industry developments, and makes quick changes. Unlike corporations, PE companies do not typically worry about interbusiness synergies that might complicate divestment decisions.

Redeployment concerns

How to use the proceeds from a possible divestment is a question that sometimes prevents managers from executing the transaction in a timely fashion. The redeployment decision—reinvest, acquire, pay debt, build cash balances, repurchase stock—should be considered separately from the analysis of whether the business still fits in your portfolio.

Competing board priorities

Boards need to balance their priorities to ensure they also provide proper stewardship of the corporate portfolio. There have been waves of urgent topics for directors in recent years: risk management after the enactment of Sarbanes-Oxley, financial system crises and instability, cyberattacks, and disruption from technology-savvy new entrants. Opportunity costs to shareholders from ineffective portfolio management can be less visible and more difficult to measure than the effects of many of these challenges.

In many companies, the board encourages senior management to rigorously review the entire business portfolio only after major inflection points, such as the arrival of a new CEO or a transformative acquisition. Rarely do executives—who are closest to the market— have an ongoing mandate to make fundamental portfolio changes in response to evolving market conditions.

Employee perceptions

One CEO—definitely in the minority—has made clear that his public company is "always for sale, either one share at a time or all at once." This may be the right approach to maximizing shareholder value, but can be unsettling for employees who think their business unit may be sold at any moment even if it's performing well.

Putting theory into practice

How can boards and CEOs overcome these barriers and implement an excellent portfolio management process? First, the performance measurement system has to encourage your people to think and act like investors. Financial metrics that focus on earning returns in excess of the cost of capital will help embed a shareholder value mindset throughout the organization. Managers need to understand that capital will be allocated not to the largest business units, but to those with the highest risk-adjusted returns and best strategic fit. This approach rewards timely, well-executed acquisitions and divestments, and penalizes leaders that hold on too long to underperformers.

Once a business is identified as a divestment candidate, companies face the challenge of motivating the unit's management to execute a transaction that will maximize value for the parent. Such motivation is especially important when the business must first be restructured or when the divestment process may take a year or longer. However, current line employees rarely have the mindset or the tool kit to do a short-term turnaround and then execute a divestment like a PE firm would. One valuable approach is to maintain a small team with these capabilities that can parachute in to help with special circumstances.

A separate but related challenge is to have compensation and career planning policies in place that recognize that those doing the turn-around may not stay with the business—or even the company—after the transaction closes. Similar to owning equity in a PE company, the team could be rewarded based on net proceeds. Beyond financial incentives, these managers might be retained by offering them new roles that provide further career development opportunities.

Paying attention to employees' anxieties helps build a culture that celebrates divestments as a necessary part of creating shareholder value. Compensation in the form of performance and "stay" bonuses plays a role, but qualitative actions are equally powerful. Leading practice companies work hard to explain the transaction's benefits to the people who will be most affected. Employees need to understand how their business will become a core focus of its new owners, and that will present personal growth opportunities. Each deal also builds (or detracts from) the seller's reputation with its remaining employees. When planning for each divestment, senior management needs to ask itself: "What can we do to positively engage our people in promoting and executing this transaction?"

The board is in a unique position to provide objective perspectives on portfolio decisions. The directors' annual strategy off-site meeting provides an excellent opportunity to examine the financial performance and strategic fit of each portfolio business. Even the largest companies can benefit from asking themselves: "What if we were acquired by a PE consortium whose sole criterion was maximizing shareholder value?" Using the off-site meeting to think through the full spectrum of possibilities for realigning the portfolio and adjusting financial policy (capital structure, dividends, and share repurchases) will help management fully prepare for today's challenges—including activist shareholders.

CEOs and CFOs can no longer afford to tie up resources in suboptimal uses. Better to employ rigorous, repeatable portfolio management processes to liberate that capital and improve financial flexibility. Tomorrow's corporate winners will be those with active and effective portfolio management processes in place to counter threats and quickly capture investment opportunities.

Notes

1. "Honeywell International Inc. Comprehensive Portfolio Review Conference Call," *Thomson Reuters StreetEvents*, 10 October 2017 (edited transcript).
2. "Honeywell Spins Off Assets as Third Point's Dan Loeb Watches," *TheStreet*, 10 October 2017.
3. Michael E. Porter, "The Five Competitive Forces That Shape Strategy," *Harvard Business Review* 86, no. 1 (January 2008), 78–93.
4. Felix Barber and Michael Goold, "The Strategic Secret of Private Equity," *Harvard Business Review* via www.hbr.org, September 2007.
5. See, for example, B. Espen Eckbo and Karin S. Thorburn, "Corporate Restructuring: Breakups and LBOs" via http://ssrn.com/abstract=1133153, May 2008.

5

Do your acquisitions consistently pay off for shareholders?

Brian Salsberg

Was it the best of times or the worst of times? In 2000, CEOs Gerald Levin and Steve Case announced that Case's America Online would be acquiring Levin's Time Warner for about US$182 billion in stock and debt. At the time, it was the largest takeover ever. Time's own *Fortune* magazine reported on the "widespread confusion about the payoff in this deal." How should Wall Street evaluate this transaction, the unprecedented acquisition of an old, storied media company by a new, digital one? Veteran journalist Carol Loomis wrote, "The murkiness won't be dispelled soon. Even at internet speed, it will take some time for the world to judge whether AOL overpaid in offering 1.5 shares of its stock for each Time Warner share, or whether Time Warner sold its impressive assets too cheaply, or whether this is truly a marriage made in heaven."[1]

Since then, the union has become the poster child for matches made in Hades. Two of AOL Time Warner's problems were the dot-com crash and then the corporate-culture clash of analog-content creators and digital-content distributors. Its stock price plummeted, and Levin left the company in 2002. The board approved the diplomatic Richard Parsons to replace him, and Parsons braced shareholders for the turnaround.[2] In a few years, he indeed helped turn the company around, dropping AOL from its name and restoring Time Warner to its perch as the world's most profitable media company.[3]

Fast-forward to 2007. Parsons's successor, Jeff Bewkes, was known for his celebrated television dramas (e.g. producing *The Sopranos*) rather than for corporate drama. His strategy focused on what he considered to be the company's competitive advantage—its video content—and he started investing more than US$12 billion a year in new program development. He also shed assets that didn't strengthen the company's competitive position, such as the remains of AOL, Time Warner's cable distribution business, and the Time Inc. magazine group. In 2017, Bewkes announced his biggest deal yet: the sale of the whole company to AT&T for US$109 billion. With the June 2018 closing of this new marriage of content and digital distribution, Bewkes has delivered an eye-popping 341% return to shareholders during his time in office, including spin-offs and dividends.[4]

An age-old M&A question

Our tale of two Time Warner deals brings us to one of the more debated questions within the world of modern finance: on average, have M&As destroyed more value than they have created? Among those who say "M&A activity generally creates shareholder value" are many investment bankers, corporate lawyers, shareholder activists, and other advisors who make their living by advocating and brokering such deals. Those who say "Such deals often fail to create value and can even destroy it" are typically management consultants who sell their postmerger integration services to forestall the predicted destruction. They often say that the main reasons for not delivering sufficient value are overpaying for the deal and missteps in integrating the acquired company. They also will add that management tends to underestimate both deal integration costs and the difficulty in capturing synergies.

To get at an empirical answer, EY reviewed much of the scholarly and not-so-scholarly research on the subject. In one study of 500 publicly traded companies in developed markets, the enterprise value growth rate of serial acquirers—those firms that acquired at least one company a year between 2009 and 2013—was 25% higher than that of firms without acquisitions. These serial acquirers had a 31% higher enterprise value to EBITDA multiple than the nonbuyers.[5] Of course, correlation is not causality, and comparing companies that do many deals with those that do fewer doesn't tell us what might have happened to these acquisitive companies had they not acquired.

Stress testing your M&A activities

Though there may not exist definitive statistical proof of M&A's value, we have seen the following, time and time again: companies that do not innovate and grow don't thrive. Instead, they slip into a rapidly accelerating death spiral of market-share erosion, brand devaluation, talent attrition, and cost cutting. This inevitably leads to a further slowdown in top-line growth, a decline in stock price (which of course is largely based on expectations of future growth), and a loss of shareholder confidence. Even those companies considered by many to be the most internally innovative and well run—Microsoft, Disney, and Johnson & Johnson, to name a few—rely to varying degrees upon M&A to fuel their innovation and growth. How could they otherwise develop all of the operational know-how, market access, customer knowledge, intellectual property, and other attributes required to succeed in this rapidly changing world? M&A is a crucial tool for growth and survival.

However, not all M&A is good; in some cases, companies move too quickly. Valeant Pharmaceutical's rapid attempt to digest more than 50 acquisitions over five years is one example. Likewise, the infamous WorldCom made 65 acquisitions in rapid succession before it imploded. But that type of roll-up strategy tends to be the exception rather than the rule.

If M&A is an essential item on a firm's Capital Agenda, then the question that board members, CEOs, CFOs, heads of corporate development, and other executive stakeholders should ask themselves is: "How do we manage the upside return and downside risk of each deal?" Put another way, "How do we stress test our M&A— particularly when we are doing many transactions—in order to maximize shareholder value?" We suggest four areas of action:

1. Choose the right deal type for your goals

Companies have many reasons to make an acquisition. We categorize these deal types into four quadrants, according to the size of the acquired company relative to the acquirer and the complexity of the business models to be integrated. See Figure 5.1.

- *Scale.* This is typically a large combination in the same or very similar product or service area. It is intended to increase sales or pricing power in the market and to gain cost synergies. Examples include the Discovery-Scripps acquisition and the Praxair-Linde merger of equals.
- *Transformation.* These acquisitions are both large enough and strategic enough to transform the company into something new and different. Steve Case and Gerald Levin said of the AOL/Time Warner deal that Time Warner would change from an analog company to a digital one through AOL's acquisition. Another example would be the Dow/DuPont merger.
- *Tuck-in.* This is a small to medium-size acquisition (relative to the size of the acquirer) in a space similar to the acquirer's core business. It fills some gap and leverages the existing base without a dramatic change to the core business. Many transactions in

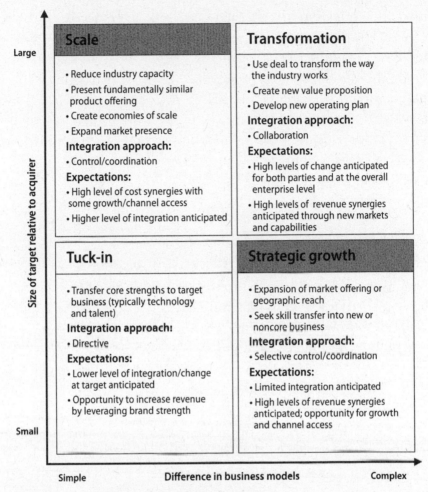

Figure 5.1 Categories of deal types

the packaged goods, personal care, and pharmaceutical space fit this category. Estée Lauder's acquisition spree, including GLAMGLOW, Le Labo, Rodin, Smashbox Beauty Cosmetics, and Too Faced, fall into this category. So does Johnson & Johnson Consumer's acquisition of NeuWave Medical for its soft tissue microwave ablation capabilities.

- *Strategic growth (also known as a bolt-on).* This is a small to medium-size acquisition in a new area, or an area different from or adjacent to the core. It is a means of diversifying while leveraging part of the same platform, infrastructure, or skill set. Examples include Microsoft/LinkedIn, Amazon/Whole Foods, and Tyson/Pierre Foods.

Deals might sometimes fall into more than one of the quadrants. What matters most is that the deal rationale aligns with the integration strategy and architecture.

2. Use objectivity in valuation and business modeling

As we discussed in Chapter 2, using objectivity prevents overpaying and allows you to plot more than one path to risk-adjusted value creation by not relying solely on a specific inorganic path to growth. It's also important to have a strong stage-gate process that is consistently applied. Investment bankers and others are incentivized to get deals done, so it's important to counterbalance that view with a risk-adjusted view of the synergies and other valuation assumptions.

3. Conduct thorough due diligence

Due diligence must thoroughly cover all the crucial areas, including the following:

- Financial.
- Tax.
- Legal and environmental.
- Commercial, including such functional areas as information technology (IT), cybersecurity, and manufacturing operations.
- Cultural fit, or the similarities and differences between organizations, especially the potential points of conflict (the review must include a plan for onboarding, socialization, and acclimation).

In our experience, thorough due diligence, with a particular focus on the future, can help remove politics and personalities from the decision process by forcing everyone involved to view the deal through the same lens—namely, one of what the operating model will look like postclose, how long it will take to get there, and what the costs and benefits are. Especially in the dynamic world we live in, due diligence must focus more on the future potential of the target than on its history leading up to the acquisition.

4. Formulate integration strategy and implementation plans, and work to ensure they're aligned to deal strategy

Too often, executives underappreciate the importance of integration strategy, the difficulty of capturing synergies, and the deterioration of value that comes from moving too slowly. This is why increasingly we see corporate boards asking for the integration playbook or plan as part of the due diligence process, and why integrations are not a one-size-fits-all effort. Rather, the best executives work with their integration leaders to align around a plan, communicate it to others, prioritize resourcing for the plan, and help troubleshoot throughout implementation.

Lessons learned

Boards are requesting more detailed integration strategies and road maps as part of their approval process. They want to know the source of synergies, a rough time line to capture value, who will drive integration, how leaders will set up the process so that it does not distract employees or detract from the business, and how it will be funded. This section will help executives to build a robust integration strategy and create that more detailed road map by focusing on five elements of a strong integration. (See Figure 5.2.)

Figure 5.2   Elements of a strong integration

Why: Vision and integration strategy

Deal makers (namely the corporate development or M&A team) need clarity in deal strategy and the expected level of integration, especially with transactions that involve capabilities outside of the buyer's core competency. If deal makers stray from their original deal thesis and rationale, they may make undesirable or suboptimal compromises during integration. It's also critical to drive toward more seamless handoffs among the corporate development team, the integration teams, and business leaders responsible for executing the integration.

Recommended actions

1. Align the executive team on the deal thesis and value proposition by articulating them in writing. Then create a set of guiding principles that are agreed to by the board and senior

management. It should contain elements that help with the many decisions to come. For example, it might spell out which brand will be kept in physical stores versus online. Such a document will eliminate a lot of noise and confusion as the integration moves ahead.

2. Keep the guiding principles document current. No integration plan survives intact by the end of Day 1 of the integration, so it's important to follow the principles when the unexpected happens; however, when major factors surface, you must modify the principles as necessary. The worst situation is to have no document, or a document that has become irrelevant and is ignored.

3. Align executives at the target firm on the deal thesis and value proposition, and get the target on board with the integration strategy and plans.

4. Do not waste precious time between signing and the close. This period may be as short as 60 days, in the case of a simple public-to-public or public-private deal requiring little or no complex regulatory and shareholder review, or up to two years in the most complex global deals. Regardless of the length of the sign-to-close window, planning and preparing for execution starting on Day 1 are essential. The use of clean teams and other mechanisms available to avoid "gun-jumping" penalties enables a robust preclosing integration process.

What: Operating model and organization design

An early and important action is to identify talent pools critical to delivering customer care. If this is not done, you can expect a host of problems that result in lost value, including increased customer dissatisfaction and attrition, and employee disengagement and retention challenges.

In addition, the lack of shared understanding of the target's cultural heritage can lead to real culture clashes during integration, with the possibility of some of these clashes being quite public. Elements of an organization's heritage are its organizational values, management style, communication style, approach to innovation, tolerance for risk taking, and other cultural markers. Lack of insight into programs, training, and benefits that support this culture may result in ineffective incentives or real pushback during integration.

We've found that the biggest drivers of integration complexity are the number of employees involved, the number of countries where operations are located, the disparity among the two companies' major information systems, and to what extent the acquired company is a carved-out business requiring transition services agreements (TSAs) and a lot of heavy lifting on Day 1. With integrations that involve thousands of employees and multiple countries, it's crucial that the integration be directed or advised by people experienced in this type of complexity. After one such integration, we took a moment to count the sum total of actions that were taken. The number was close to 10,000. Given the relatively short integration windows that most organizations work under, experienced guidance is a key determinant of success.

Recommended actions

1. Form and maintain a clear view of what the new combined entity should look like, and be involved in all early key decisions.
2. Conduct a coordinated organization-design and talent-selection process that leads to robust onboarding and retention planning.
3. Design the operating model with policies and procedures that foster the desired combined culture and address culture flashpoints.
4. Do not merely integrate if you can transform. Integrations can serve as a trigger event to begin a more fundamental transformation of a company. There is an important difference

between integrating (putting two things together) and transforming (rewiring or replatforming and reshaping). A transformation must be a deliberate decision. It means that the acquiring company needs to look as much at itself as it does at the target. This is not easy, but it's a rare opportunity to be able to effect significant change.

Who: Integration management office and governance

Leaders from both the buyer and the target firms must show their continuous commitment to the integration process. They can do this by being visible and active at steering committee meetings, helping to make critical decisions, communicating frequently, and participating in frequently asked questions sessions.

It is not an overstatement to say that integrations succeed or fail because of the chemistry among people and their actions (or inactions). Finance, taxation, operations, and many other factors are highly important, but the people dimension is crucial.

Culture does not change easily, and it does not change with mere words, however true or sincere you make those words. Actions are what count, and words without actions are worse than no words at all.

Recommended actions

1. Select key integration leaders early, and don't be afraid to make changes if needed. Get them involved during due diligence and keep them involved moving forward.
2. Engage with leaders of the target to define processes and refine what has worked in the past for their organization.
3. Identify individuals to fill roles within the integration governance structure; group members into teams; clearly define those roles, responsibilities, and decision rights; and clearly articulate which decisions each level of the governance structure should make.

4. You have a very small window to make tone-setting changes; they must happen right at the outset of the integration. Examples of actions that make people sit up and take notice are a key promotion of someone in the target company, or a "ceremonial hanging" or dismissal of a counterproductive faction leader.

How: Change management and communications

At any point, people can lose sight of objectives and slip out of alignment, jeopardizing business continuity, value preservation, and the employee experience. Leaders from both the buy side and the sell side must align their messages, coordinate their delivery, and sustain a consistent, well-coordinated internal and external messaging campaign for the duration of the integration. Such a thoughtful campaign minimizes confusion, frustration, and flight risks among employees, and preserves the value of both the brand and the deal. The more complex a transaction, the more extensive and frequent must be the communications.

It's helpful to remember that in most acquisitions, a relative handful of people are on the integration team. They know all about the deal, what it involves, and what it does not involve. At the same time, the vast majority of people in both organizations typically hear and transmit constant rumors.

Recommended actions

1. Don't underestimate the importance of regular, clear, and motivating communications in cultural change. Here's a handy way to think about communication: at the point when you think you have overcommunicated and are simply repeating messages, that's usually when you are just getting to the right level of sharing information. If employees are standing around the watercooler trying to speculate about a question you have not

addressed, that means they are not spending that time building the business.

2. Align messages to critical themes aimed at each stakeholder group. For example, employees will want to understand how the merger might affect their jobs and their benefits packages. If that information is not yet available, then say so.

3. Remember to include all supplier relationships in critical communications. This includes not just part-timers and independent contractors, but also temporary staffing agencies and technical service providers.

4. Develop an employee notification process to stage and coordinate the delivery of these messages, including who should deliver which messages—managers, investor relations, or human resources (HR) professionals.

How much: Value creation and synergies

Revenue synergies may be more central to the value proposition for a transaction than cost synergies; however, they may require significant investment and a longer lead time to realize. Lack of comprehensive due diligence efforts may result in unexpected costs. An example is insufficient due diligence on IT assets, specifically the condition and age of the assets, complexity of design, transferability of licenses and security, and stability of the infrastructure. In general, companies often underestimate, or don't bother to take the time to model the cost of achieving synergies. EY uses a standard of 0.5–1.5 times the recurring annual cost synergies to estimate one-time integration costs.

Recommended actions

1. Demand analytical rigor and insight into value creation and synergies, as well as clarity on capturing them.

2. Define cost-reduction and cost-avoidance opportunities to help achieve synergies in the short term.

3. Conduct thorough due diligence, particularly a comprehensive audit of IT systems on the dimensions of age, condition, complexity of design, transferability of licenses, and the security, stability, and adaptability of the infrastructure.

4. When you analyze the crucial staffing question, be sure to ask about "contingent staff" (i.e., contractors) and also people on leaves of absence. There have been documented cases where an acquisition involved several thousand people in this classification, yet they had not originally been included in the head count.

5. Thoroughly vet the baseline assumptions and measurement metrics used in the quantification of synergy amounts, and understand sensitivities and interdependencies associated with IT or other capital expenditures.

6. Engage integration team members from both buyer and target to align everyone on synergy metrics and time line, and assign responsibility for integrating people, processes, and technology.

7. Translate the value proposition into financial and operational metrics to include in the integration plan at a functional level. Clearly define the baseline and targets for improvement within a reasonable time frame within the integration team.

8. Establish a rigorous synergy program with clear individual accountabilities to accelerate and exceed targets, and consider striking a balance between both revenue and cost synergies. Make sure accountability is at a high level (e.g. a direct report to the CFO).

9. Study the assumptions and expectations behind synergy targets to get a feel for their achievability under a range of scenarios.

10. Take the top-down synergy number and validate those synergies from the bottom up with owners early. Assign individual accountability not only for each synergy target, but also for interim targets. This helps to ensure that you stay on pace to realize the overall synergy goal.

11. Develop a robust plan for the one-time investments required to achieve the targets, especially for revenue and growth, and include a realistic schedule of capital expenditures.

Notes

1. Carol J. Loomis with Christine Chen, "AOL + TWX = ??? Do the math, and you might wonder if this company's long-term annual return to investors can beat a Treasury bond's," *Fortune*, 7 February 2000. Web, 5 May 2017. http://archive.fortune.com/magazines/fortune/fortune_archive/2000/02/07/272827/index.htm

2. Johnnie L. Roberts, "New Leadership at Time Warner?" *Newsweek*, 25 October 2007. Web, 5 May 2017. http://www.newsweek.com/new-leadership-time-warner-103781.

3. Irene Hall, "Richard Parsons: Just as the Closing Credits Rolled, Time Warner Worked a Miracle," *The Independent*, 5 December 2004. Web, 5 May 2017. www.independent.co.uk/news/business/analysis-and-features/Richard-parsons-just-as-the-closing-credits-rolled-time-warner-worked-a-miracle-752832.html.

4. "Time Warner's Boss Is the Anti-mogul," *The Economist*, 8 April 2017.

5. Greg Schooley and Mike Phillips, "Build Your M&A Muscle: Why Serial Acquirers Win at Value Creation," AT Kearney, 2015. https://www.atkearney.com/mergers-acquisitions/article?/a/build-your-m-a-muscle-why-serial-acquirers-win-at-value-creation.

6

Are you planning and executing divestments for maximum value?

Paul Hammes and Subin Baral

On the heels of a major acquisition, a global medical technology services company began considering a potential carve-out. The options were either to invest more in the business in order to meet regulatory requirements, or to sell to someone else. Management decided to divest because the business had limited long-term growth potential and was inconsistent with the company's core operations and strategy.

All aspects of the unit were carefully considered, particularly customer overlap with other parts of the portfolio, as well as its significant revenue and earnings contributions. To determine exactly which package of assets would be most attractive to potential buyers, the seller examined four different deal perimeters, carefully crafting a value story for each. Adding to the carve-out's complexity: the business's activities in finance, tax, information technology, and operations were interdependent with the parent across 50 countries.

Significant up-front separation planning across key functions began 8 months before signing and 11 months before close. This thorough preparation allowed the seller to continue to focus on running the business and maintaining its value along the way. The unit not only attracted both corporate and private equity buyers, but also garnered a price 12% above initial expectations. Though many complex carve-out transactions take well over one year, this transaction occurred within a tight 11-month time line, was highly successful, and provided much needed capital for debt repayment and future acquisitions.

Divesting is critical to your capital strategy

Divestments should be a fundamental part of your Capital Agenda, especially in a volatile and disruptive environment where you need to fund growth and essential innovation. In our experience, most companies act too slowly and hold on to assets too long. Monetizing noncore and underperforming businesses helps companies redeploy resources to invest in digital capabilities, expand product ranges, and broaden geographic footprints.

Divestments can be an efficient route to unlocking hidden shareholder value, because they generate cash and often lead to an improved share price for the remaining company—if done well. External forces, including geopolitical uncertainty, macroeconomic volatility, technology-driven risks and opportunities, regulatory changes, and shareholder activism, can also spark divestment discussions. Such external forces will continue to drive divestments for the foreseeable future.

What defines a successful divestment?

Before delving into the mechanics of divesting, let's define what we consider success. On one level the goal is to achieve your strategic imperatives; but to get more specific, we use these core criteria:

Maximize sale price

Based on our research and observations, almost half of divestments fail to realize sufficient value for their shareholders because companies tend to underprepare, and then focus too much on speed to close. It's a costly mistake to get into the mindset of "We need to just get rid of it!"

Close the deal quickly

Our research shows companies are 60% more likely to beat their sale price expectations when they prioritize value over speed.[1] Although managing the trade-off between speed and value can be critical, it is usually a false trade-off. Many companies rush to get the deal done, but in the process cut corners during preparation. As a result, the deal takes longer to close and its value declines, because potential buyers have less faith in the value story. Sellers are much more likely to maximize their sale price and shorten deal duration when they take time up front to prepare the business for sale.

Achieve an enhanced valuation multiple for the remaining company

Just as the buyer wants reinforcement that the purchase was a good decision, the seller's confirmation of a good decision is manifested in a strong valuation multiple for the remaining company.

Divestment guiding principles

Successful sellers understand that carving out a business is typically far more complex than acquiring one. Executing a divestment requires planning, effort, and urgency. "Thinking like a buyer" helps you control and expedite the process, as well as maximize value. These guiding principles should be applied before marketing commences:

1. *Define the perimeter of the transaction early.* Which components are included and excluded? Should the business be sold as a

whole, or split and offered to multiple buyers? Though the perimeter often changes, this is a cornerstone of the planning process because it can affect all other carve-out work. The key is to remain flexible and agile as the deal evolves.

2. *Fully consider transaction alternatives.* Companies should explore alternative structures to achieve the optimal transaction outcome. Though every divestment will have unique features, most transaction types fall into four main categories, as shown in Figure 6.1. Further, companies often dual-track transaction structures to maximize value for their stakeholders—pursuing both a spin-off to public investors and a third-party sale—until a clearly superior option emerges.

3. *Develop a buyer mindset.* By doing so, sellers can better understand value drivers and consequently tailor information to maximize value while shortening the divestment process. Figure 6.2 describes focus areas for both strategic and private equity buyers. Sellers must identify and understand their pool of potential buyers to evaluate their purchase and valuation perspectives. Then they must provide a comprehensive plan for how the unit will be operationally separated from the parent and fit into the buyer's portfolio. For example, PE buyers usually are interested in a stand-alone basis whereas strategic buyers care about the synergistic view.

4. *Plan for separation early.* Successful sellers understand that unanticipated separation issues can lower the value to potential buyers who desire a functional business. The appropriate governance structure—with representation from the board of directors, corporate development, finance, tax, operations, human resources, legal, and investor relations—supports the creation of an appropriate project plan with key milestones throughout the divestment life cycle. Rigorous planning and adherence to processes will help sellers avoid value-destroying surprises.

   To illustrate: on a quarterly investor call, a CFO committed to a closing date for a significant spin-off without checking on feasibility with the deal execution team.

	Carve-out and sale	Spin	Reverse Morris trust (RMT)	Joint venture
Description	• Partial separation and sale of a business or assets to a third party	• Contributions of assets/businesses into a separate publicly traded NewCo to existing shareholders	• Spin-off of a company that is subsequently acquired as part of plan—shareholders of distributing company must retain greater than 50% interest in SpinCo directly or indirectly	• Contribute assets/business (equity) into a new entity with a business partner
Average duration	• 6 to 9 months to signing	• 9 to 15 months to stand alone after an effective spin	• 9 to 15 months to stand alone after an effective RMT	• 6 to 12 months after finding a joint venture partner

Advantages	• Speed of execution
	• Preserve confidentiality
	• Minimum business interruption
	• Flexibility to change course
	• Disposal of assets that no longer strategically align or perform
	• Less complex to execute (compared to other alternatives)
	• Attracts the most potential buyers
	• Stimulates sense of competition among buyers
	• Multiple options for seller
		• Raise capital while restructuring debt
		• Monetize interest prior to spin-off
		• Stock is distributed (not purchased)
		• Avoid perception property is "shopped"
		• No taxable gain
		• Improved management focus
		• Retain relationship with business
			• Maintain some confidentiality
			• Stimulate sense of competition among buyers
			• Multiple options for seller
			• Reduced valuation risk because the exchange includes established value
			• Improved management focus
			• Retain relationship with business
				• Enhance a business by adding the right strategic partner
				  ○ Faster growth and profit opportunity
				  ○ Access to new markets, relationships, and technology
				  ○ Increased capacity
				• Leverage each partner's strengths to minimize weaknesses
				• Shared risk exposure and capital investment
				• Retain relationship with business
				• Tailored to fit your needs (life span, charter)

Disadvantages	• May not realize maximum value • Will not reach full potential universe of buyers • Transition service agreements longer term (and potentially operate at a loss) • Taxable transaction	• Requires substantial top-level management time commitment • Qualification requirements to achieve tax-free spin-off • Cost to restructure debt • Longer timetable • Public company costs/reporting burdens • Stand-alone considerations • Financial markets impact deal	• A limited universe of prospective buyers • Delay in execution • Risk of access to confidential material by "tire kickers" • Some business disruption • Regulatory approvals • Financial markets impact deal	• Partners may not share same vision • Frequently have unequitable contributions (knowledge, resources, investments) • Complex structure • Risks if partners have different cultures (commingling of management styles) • Partners have to agree on an up-front exit strategy

Figure 6.1   Transaction structuring considerations

During the separation process, the company discovered regulatory hurdles in numerous countries that delayed the transaction by six months. The company's stock lost more than 20% of its value post announcement and did not recoup its losses until well after separation.

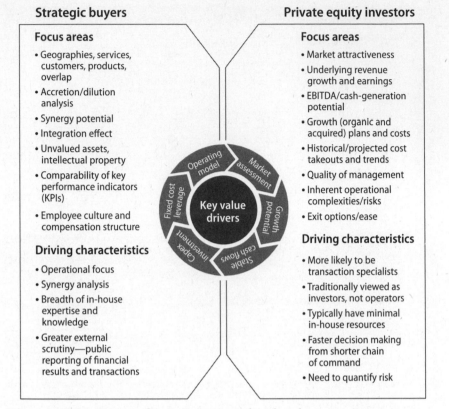

Strategic buyers

Focus areas

- Geographies, services, customers, products, overlap
- Accretion/dilution analysis
- Synergy potential
- Integration effect
- Unvalued assets, intellectual property
- Comparability of key performance indicators (KPIs)
- Employee culture and compensation structure

Driving characteristics

- Operational focus
- Synergy analysis
- Breadth of in-house expertise and knowledge
- Greater external scrutiny—public reporting of financial results and transactions

Private equity investors

Focus areas

- Market attractiveness
- Underlying revenue growth and earnings
- EBITDA/cash-generation potential
- Growth (organic and acquired) plans and costs
- Historical/projected cost takeouts and trends
- Quality of management
- Inherent operational complexities/risks
- Exit options/ease

Driving characteristics

- More likely to be transaction specialists
- Traditionally viewed as investors, not operators
- Typically have minimal in-house resources
- Faster decision making from shorter chain of command
- Need to quantify risk

Key value drivers — Operating model, Market assessment, Growth potential, Stable cash flows, Capex/Investment, Fixed cost leverage

Figure 6.2   Buyer focus areas and criteria

5. *Address all stakeholders.* Do not leave employees in the dark to imagine what may happen and thereby risk losing key talent. Involve individuals with mission-critical knowledge and capabilities early on to help you make the most informed decisions. Though this may seem obvious, the reality is that often the very people who really know the business to be divested are not included early enough, often because of concerns over confidentiality. Clearly communicate the strategic rationale behind the divestment and its intended effect on shareholder value. Don't forget about external stakeholders, whether they

be shareholders, creditors, customers, or vendors. Frequent communications instill confidence.

Leading sources of value erosion

- Operating performance deteriorates, undermining your value story.
- Incomplete due diligence materials reduce buyers' willingness to bid competitively.
- Lack of flexibility in transaction structuring fails to attract optimal buyer group.
- Inadequate resources are devoted to executing the transaction.
- Insufficiently developed and documented stand-alone costs scare off financial buyers.
- Tax due diligence and planning fail to anticipate needs of each buyer group.
- Missed opportunities to fix or improve the business before the sale suppress value.
- Senior management commits publicly to an unachievable closing date.

Can you increase business value before divesting?

We often hear executives say, "It doesn't make sense to invest in a business we are going to sell." On the contrary: when a company begins to explore strategic alternatives, the highest priorities for any seller should be to strengthen the business, develop the equity story, and execute on a seamless separation. This requires you to regularly evaluate trade-offs between initiatives to improve the business and their associated costs.

Value enhancements come in two flavors: those you can implement before beginning the divestment process, and those you don't make but can credibly describe to potential buyers. For this second category, sellers should demonstrate a road map so a buyer can execute on the improvement plan. Some ways to create value include:

- *Treat the business as a stand-alone entity*. Sellers encourage buyer confidence when they can provide separate financial and operating results for a to-be-divested business. When a business has been earmarked for sale, sellers should explore the feasibility of internally reorganizing to put the business on a stand-alone basis. Key focus areas include:
  - Go-to-market models, such as direct versus distributors.
  - Financial reporting, including balance sheets, income statements, working capital, and forecasts.
  - Rational cost allocations or, better yet, direct costs.
  - Appropriately capitalized legal entities.
  - Legal and regulatory requirements in applicable countries, particularly those that may prohibit a buyer from operating the business on the desired closing date.
- *Enhance revenue*. Although an extensive product expansion program may be unrealistic for a business for sale, companies can start to optimize their product footprint across customers and geographies. A bolder move is to add products or expand into different geographies or markets through a joint venture arrangement, or to consider acquiring another company. A global private equity fund completed several bolt-on acquisitions to bolster its real estate portfolio: it acquired commercial estate to expand in geographies and also a carved-out business of a large corporation to add size and scale to the asset.
- *Extract working capital*. Buyers generally won't pay for excess working capital. Companies planning to divest a business need only enough working capital to run the business on a day-to-day basis. Any amount beyond that should be liberated prior to beginning the divestment process and put to work elsewhere, as we discuss extensively in Chapter 8.

- *Cut costs through procurement.* Companies can enter into group-purchasing agreements, or even form their own buyer consortium to reduce costs and enhance margins.

What does it take to close the deal and maximize value?

Most companies do not divest as often as they acquire and don't recognize that divestments are complex and require thoughtful governance, resourcing, and prioritization across all functions. The activities of the tax, financial, and operational separation work streams must be prioritized against competing initiatives within the organization. Figure 6.3 contains a brief overview of a typical divestment work plan. While this chapter covers divestments of all types, here we'll focus in detail on carve-out transactions as an important example.

Let's look at each of the essential focus areas.

Governance. Executing a successful deal without undermining core business operations

Leadership needs to establish a governance structure that defines the transaction time line, milestones, roles, and responsibilities. The separation management office (SMO) should have representation from the entire enterprise, including tax, finance, supply chain, IT, human resources, legal, and communications. With the SMO in place, each team must be appropriately resourced with those best positioned to execute, not simply those who are available. This often entails a combination of internal and external resources.

Tax. Structuring the deal to minimize tax risks

We often hear, "There is little benefit to tax planning when we don't know who the buyer is." This can be a costly mistake: tax issues can make or break a deal because of their economic effects on both seller and buyer. Our research indicates the majority of sellers neglect to

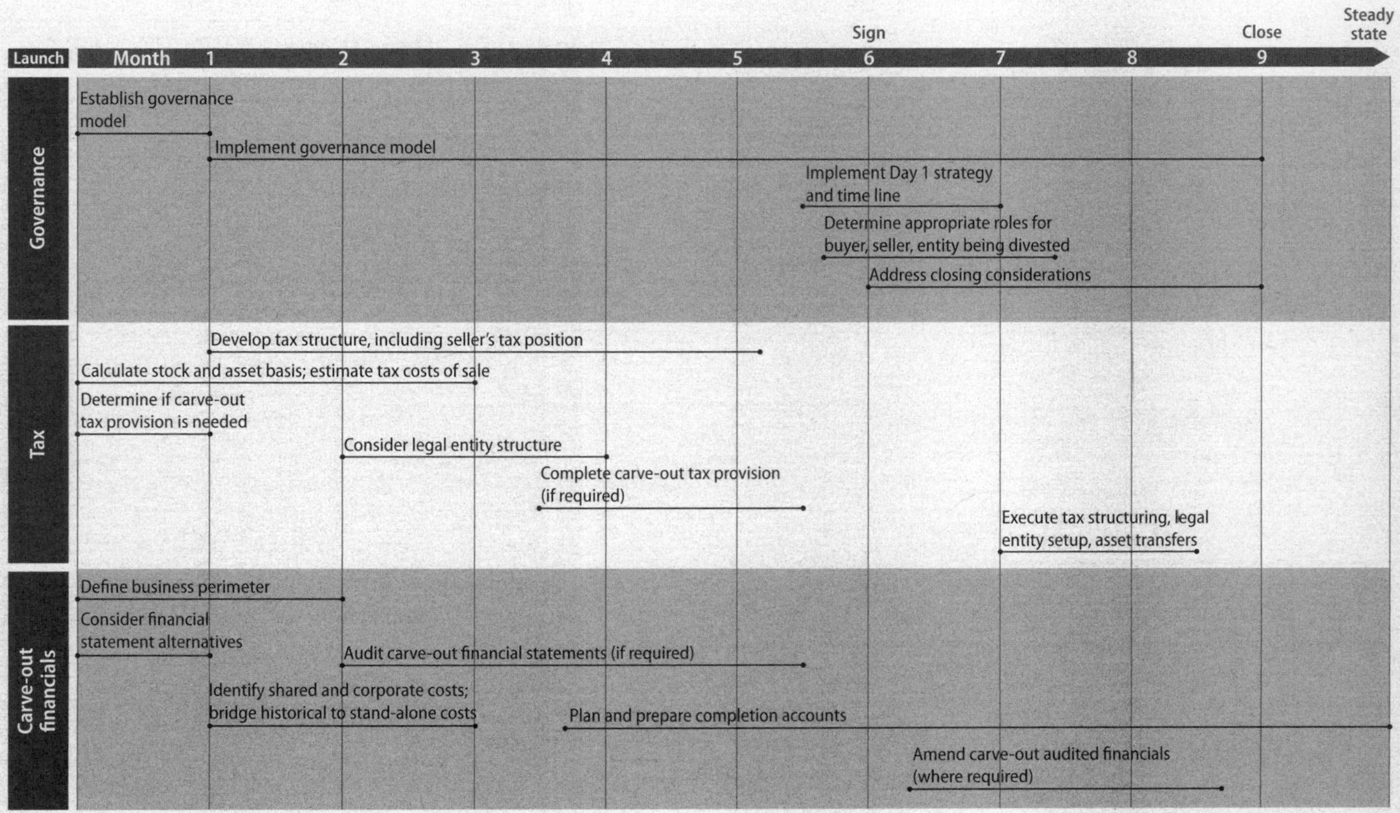

Figure 6.3 Divestment work plan

The figure is a divestment work plan presented as a timeline chart spanning Month 1 through Steady state (with milestones labeled Launch, Sign, Close). Rows are grouped into three workstreams:

Governance
- Establish governance model
- Implement governance model

Tax
- Develop tax structure, including seller's tax position
- Calculate stock and asset basis; estimate tax costs of sale
- Determine if carve-out tax provision is needed
- Consider legal entity structure
- Complete carve-out tax provision (if required)
- Implement Day 1 strategy and time line
- Determine appropriate roles for buyer, seller, entity being divested
- Address closing considerations
- Execute tax structuring, legal entity setup, asset transfers

Carve-out financials
- Define business perimeter
- Consider financial statement alternatives
- Identify shared and corporate costs; bridge historical to stand-alone costs
- Audit carve-out financial statements (if required)
- Plan and prepare completion accounts
- Amend carve-out audited financials (where required)

Timeline header: Month | 1 | 2 | 3 | 4 | 5 | 6 | 7 | 8 | 9 | Steady state; with Launch at start, Sign near month 6, Close near month 9.

90

Figure 6.3 Divestment work plan (*continued*)

	Month	1	2	3	4	5	6	7	8	9	Steady state
		Launch					Sign			Close	

Deal-basis information
- Develop value story and prepare for buyers
- Compile deal-basis information; present normalized EBITDA
- Prepare and issue sell-side due diligence report
- Develop forecast and value drivers
- Compile working capital and debt-like items for contract positioning
- Develop view of stand-alone and one-time costs
- Estimate purchase price settlements
- Monitor financial results and synergy realization vs. forecast

Operational separation
- Define current-state operating model
- Assess time required to establish new legal entities
- Define future operating model for the business and separation strategy
- Scale organization size and establish process to transfer employees
- Define TSA requirements and service delivery model
- Initiate separation planning; begin mobilizing resources
- Mitigate stranded costs; align the mitigation with TSA exit planning
- Tailor the communications strategy to each constituent
- Execute separation plan
- Plan to operationalize new legal entities
- Close works council and union negotiations (where required)
- Stabilize business and deliver; exit TSAs

91

effectively communicate tax upsides to bidders, thereby failing to maximize value. The most successful sellers consider tax early in the process, and proactively consider the tax needs of possible types of bidders—corporate versus private equity, domestic versus foreign. Enhancing a transaction's tax structure requires detailed knowledge of historical tax risks and upsides, as well as an understanding of how to mitigate tax costs while maximizing upsides to benefit both the buyer and the seller. See Chapter 9. Some essential practices:

- *Ensure tax, finance, and corporate development are aligned* with the deal-basis financial statements to ensure that the right information drives critical decisions.
- *Determine which legal entities will be sold as stock versus assets*, and calculate tax gain or loss. The anticipated tax bill may drive a "go/no-go" decision and help to focus on how to maximize after-tax proceeds.
- *Consider a legal entity structure* that helps drive value for a buyer by optimizing taxes on sale and repatriation of proceeds, as well as future operating earnings.
- *Anticipate required tax provisions.* Will full generally accepted accounting principles (GAAP)–compliant financial statements be needed, or will bidders accept special-purpose or abbreviated statements?

Some examples of common tax-efficient divestment strategies:

- *Tax-free spin-off.* An existing business is separated out of a company. Shares in the spin-off entity are distributed directly to the company's existing shareholders. When appropriately planned and structured, sellers can divest appreciated assets without incurring US federal income tax.
- *Reverse Morris Trust (RMT).* A number of companies, particularly in technology, in recent years have completed RMT transactions, allowing for a tax-free spin-off of the business

followed by a third-party acquisition of a minority interest in the spun-off entity. These structures apply only in specific fact patterns, but in the right scenario they allow sellers to monetize a significant portion of their ownership interest without incurring tax.

Carve-out financials. Preparing for the buyer pool and their financial requirements

Carve-out financial statements, whether on a deal basis, audited, or both, are paramount to the success of any divestment. We often hear, "Existing information will satisfy any deal-basis financial statements," or "Why prepare audited financial statements? Most buyers don't require them," or "They can get a waiver." Here are some counterarguments:

- Does your internal financial information reflect the anticipated perimeter of the transaction and related operations? If not, how will prospective buyers understand the assets, liabilities, and working capital to be transferred? How will they understand the cost structure they will assume? How will the tax team determine the appropriate structure and gain/loss on the sale?
- Does your buyer pool include private equity buyers? If so, audited financial statements are typically required.
- Will your buyers, whether corporate or PE, require debt or equity financing? If so, audited financial statements are also likely required.

Although preparing financial statements for a divestment is time-consuming—three or more months for deal-basis financials and nine months or more for audited financials—deficient statements can easily derail your deal.

Figure 6.4 illustrates types of transaction-related financial statements and their triggers.

Type	Audit required	Trigger(s)	Years required	Contents	Other considerations
Deal-basis	N	Any sale	N/A. Typically 3 years of historical information (third year often TTM vs. calendar)	BS and IS, with no formal SCF, along with schedules to support diligence (e.g. quality of earnings)	If audited FS required, still need bridge to deal-basis FS
Abbreviated carve-out	Y	SEC significance rules for public registrant buyer	1–3 (based on SEC 3-05 rules)	BS and IS (SCF, if practicable), with applicable footnotes	Direct assets, liabilities, income, and expenses (need SEC preclearance)
Special purpose	Y	Buyer pool requires an audit, but not for public filing (e.g. lending or internal approval purposes)	1–3 (based on agreement with buyers)	BS, IS, SCF, statement of changes in equity and footnotes	Best for site/business with principally dedicated FS; can avoid CO matters not impacting deal (e.g. tax provision, corporate overhead, purchase accounting, and debt push down)
Regulation S-X Rule 3-05	Y	SEC significance rules for public registrant buyer or PE buyer that intends near-term IPO or to use public debt to finance acquisition (144A)	1–3, plus applicable interim periods (reviewed)	BS, IS, SCF, statement of changes in equity and footnotes	Opening BS needed for year prior to first IS presented
S-1/Form 10	Y	Carve-out IPO (S-1) Tax-free spin (Form 10) Reverse Morris Trust	3 years, plus applicable interim periods (reviewed) and earliest 2 years for "front section" of filing	BS, IS, SCF, statement of changes in equity and footnotes; MD&A, risk factors, etc.	Earliest 2 years unaudited, but on same basis as CO FS

- Financial statements (FS)
- Balance sheet (BS)
- Income statement (IS)
- Statement of cash flows (SCF)
- Carve-out (CO)
- Private equity (PE)
- Trailing twelve months (TTM)
- Management discussion & analysis (MD&A)

Figure 6.4   Financial statement requirements

Despite the extra effort required, audited financials can support a bigger buyer pool, increase competitive tension, and enhance valuation. Identifying the potential buyer pool needs to happen as early as possible.

Deal-basis information. The key elements of a strong value story

Deal–basis financial information should represent a summary of those assets, liabilities, working capital, and operations anticipated to transfer to buyers. They will be subject to extensive due diligence and form the basis for bidders' valuation analysis.

- *Define the perimeter of the business* and how it might be packaged; identify the optional components that may later be included or excluded.
- *Use the governance structure to align the deal teams* with the perimeter so there are no surprises later in the process.
- *Perform defensive due diligence on the financial statement components.* Are amounts direct? Do they contain allocations? Will they withstand buyer scrutiny?
- *Bridge the deal-basis and audited financial statements.* There generally are significant differences, and being able to articulate those to potential buyers will enhance your credibility as a seller and help facilitate the sale.

Provide a Compelling Value Story

Buyers want a due diligence package that delivers a strong value story and links historical results with operational forecasts. They'll expect a comprehensive, self-service virtual data room that supports buyer confidence in the numbers. The following are some critical steps to take:

- *Develop the divestment rationale,* anticipate buyers' value drivers, and tailor materials to support their needs.
- *Compile deal-basis information* that includes normalized EBITDA so buyers can index purchase price to an EBITDA multiple.
- *Create a view of stand-alone and one-time costs that can withstand buyer scrutiny.* This helps influence buyers' assumptions about operating model, potential synergies, and projections.

- *Prepare a sell-side due diligence report.* A well-prepared and comprehensive seller due diligence report will help enhance competition and expedite buyers' analyses.

A supportable investment thesis and deal-basis financials help maintain your credibility and control in the negotiation process. A counterexample: a global manufacturer was negotiating to sell its noncore business to a private equity firm. Although the seller prepared deal-basis financial information, it did not provide an estimate of stand-alone costs. During the negotiation, the buyer put forth its own calculations of normalized EBITDA with stand-alone and one-time costs. Its sustainable profitability assumptions were significantly lower than the seller's would have been, resulting in a considerable reduction to the offer price. Negotiations dragged on, and ultimately both parties walked away from the transaction.

Operational separation. Planning for a speedy close

We often hear, "It doesn't make sense to begin planning for the separation of the business until we have a buyer." On the contrary, rigorous up-front planning must start well before identifying a buyer, to ensure a timely closing and deliver a functioning business on Day 1. Starting early provides a much clearer view of the key decision points and enables you to minimize disruption, reduce complexity and cost, shorten the time between sign and close, and reduce the scope of transition services agreements (TSAs) and transition manufacturing agreements (TMAs).

Leading-edge separation planning begins with analyzing commingled services to enable early development of TSAs/TMAs and stranded costs modeling. Identifying long lead-time separation activities helps avoid delays in the deal time line. For example, IT is often the most entangled functional area and the one that requires the most lead time, and it is typically the most expensive to separate. As part of setting up your SMO, establish a dynamic talent management process that provides the right resources for each work stream, but also supports the day-to-day needs of the business.

Design the operating model

A credible separation strategy shows buyers the business can be separated without loss of value. This includes defining both current and future operating models. Although the buyer will eventually stand up all the functions, you'll likely need to provide transitional support in order to hand over a fully operational business. Understanding the buyer's future-state operating model allows you to identify long lead-time items—such as establishing new legal entities—and provide the service delivery model for Day 1.

In addition to separation complexity, the time line will be driven by the buyer's capabilities and desired closing date. Buyer and seller should understand and fully discuss lead times to address closing conditions such as antitrust, works council, and other regulatory approvals. This allows both parties to develop work-around solutions to meet the closing conditions on schedule. For example, market authorization requirements often require an interim operating model for Day 1 with the buyer.

Define TSA requirements

Seller and buyer also need to align on guiding principles, including an approach to separating each function. Agreeing early about the delivery model for transition services will help both understand their costs to operate on Day 1. They will also be better able to plan for exiting TSAs. A proactive approach allows the seller to identify and plan for remediating stranded costs.

Finalize work-arounds for long lead-time separation activities

Understanding long lead-time items early is crucial because the post-signing period rarely includes sufficient time to begin and complete key activities. For example, requirements to establish new legal entities vary widely and can take more than a year to fulfill. Failure to move quickly can delay establishing bank accounts, contracting with vendors, configuring systems, and selling products, all of which can postpone closing. It is critical to determine IT requirements to put new legal entities into operation, segregate data and access, address name changes, and enable separate financial reporting.

An example of effective planning: a global equipment manufacturer determined that one of its business units was not core to its future strategy. Even though a final decision had not been made to divest, management began addressing long lead-time separation activities to facilitate an exit and minimize the need for TSAs, which would distract from running its core business. Key steps included establishing new legal entities in countries where existing operations were commingled with the parent, cloning the current enterprise resource planning (ERP) system hosted by a third party, and arranging contracts with external service providers for payroll and similar services.

When a decision was made a year later to sell the business unit, the private equity buyer had confidence in the ability of the business unit to stand alone, resulting in a simplified operational due diligence process and a quick closing. The seller concluded that the up-front costs to implement these changes were more than justified by the sale proceeds, early close, and minimal TSAs requested by the buyer.

Divesting for value

In an age of market disruptions and impatient shareholders, strong divesting capabilities should be part of every company's Capital

Agenda tool kit. The first bulwark against value erosion is rigorous portfolio reviews. Perhaps the most value-damaging action a company can take is holding on to an asset too long.

Once you decide to divest, thinking like a buyer is critical to success. Sale preparation is vital, even for the best-performing unit. Flexibility around the deal perimeter and structure can be the ultimate path to success. Start operational planning early in the process to accelerate speed to close while creating value for both seller and buyer.

Even after a successful divestment, significant opportunities exist for enhancing the value of the remaining business. Once TSAs expire, certain costs aren't passed through and remain stranded with the seller. Stranded-costs management is one of the greatest challenges for the remaining business. Proper separation planning and execution will allow sellers to identify and remediate the stranded costs.

Notes

1. EY Global Corporate Divestment Study 2017, based on responses of 900 global corporate executives, offering statistical analysis of divestment priorities and reported performance on sale price of their most recent divestment.

7 | Do your financing choices support flexibility and efficiency?

K.C. Brechnitz

Before Henry Kravis could pull off the biggest leveraged buyout (LBO) in history at the time—the 1988 acquisition of RJR Nabisco for US$25 billion—he and his deal makers had to have a strategy for the capital structure of the company. They knew that most corporate loan and bond agreements contain provisions that require redemption of the debt in the event of a change in control. Hence, the LBO would wipe the slate clean of RJR Nabisco's capital structure so that Kohlberg Kravis Roberts & Co. (KKR) could start from scratch.

Kravis is one of the founders of legendary buyout firm KKR. He and his bankers at Drexel Burnham Lambert must have asked themselves what the defining characteristics of that business were. The maker of cigarettes, Oreo cookies, and Ritz crackers certainly exhibited low earnings volatility commensurate with its strong position in a stable food and cigarette market. It also had a fairly low level of capital expenditures, strong free cash flow, a moderate growth profile, and a portfolio of discrete brands that not only were valuable but could be sold off separately.

They also analyzed RJR Nabisco management's intermediate and long-term plans for the business. With the high debt levels needed to effect the acquisition, RJR Nabisco's future would not be business as usual, and managers would have to revise these plans. Indeed, KKR intended to sell off numerous parts of the business after closing the deal. Those asset sales were a key factor influencing the design of the capital structure. KKR planned to use the sale proceeds to deleverage the business. A capital structure heavy in bonds would cause value leakage in a repayment scenario, given the call premiums typically associated with redeeming bonds early. In the end, KKR and Drexel Burnham Lambert crafted a capital structure with an optimal mix of loans and bonds that not only provided much-needed operating flexibility and market depth, but also allowed for postclosing business restructuring.

Use capital structure to facilitate business goals

Corporate executives should understand the need for a capital structure to facilitate rather than inhibit the goals and objectives of a business. Yet, too many companies find themselves with a capital structure that either complicates the attraction of new capital or prohibits certain critical business activities.

How does this happen? Sometimes it's a significant unforeseen change in the business or marketplace, like a disruptive technology or an economic collapse. More often it's a nondeliberate, reactionary approach to building the capital structure. Many companies have less information and experience than do their advisors, and this asymmetry can lead to suboptimal decisions. Corporate executives sometimes react to ideas from bankers, lawyers, or board members and find themselves entering into one-off transactions that seemed appropriate at the time—but later turn out to be mistakes.

Assess your business through the capital lens

Managers can improve their capital structure decisions if they commit to a detailed business review process through the *capital lens*. As a group, they must thoroughly review their operations, marketplace, stakeholders, and the long-term strategy of the business. They need to understand how capital structure and the capital markets affect each of these elements. To arrive at an optimal capital structure, they then must explore ways to match the key characteristics of the business and its strategy with those of possible capital instruments in current capital market conditions.

The process that Henry Kravis and Drexel Burnham Lambert likely went through as they considered financing the acquisition of RJR Nabisco doesn't differ much from what companies should undergo in the absence of a potential LBO. However, businesses and the industries in which they operate are unique, and the capital structures that support them should differ accordingly. Access to capital is essential to any business: the easier it is to obtain and the lighter the burden it places on a company, the more managers can use it to fuel growth. Some businesses are capital intensive; others are people intensive. Some are global; others are local. Certain industries are more volatile; others are more stable, and yet others are seasonal. Some companies have growing capital expenditure plans, and others plan to spend amounts consistent with prior years.

Certainly the management team should understand these aspects of the company's capital needs, but managers don't often map these aspects against the opportunities and limitations of capital instruments and capital markets. As a result, a company's capital structure may come with hidden risks and hidden opportunity costs.

The first exercise you should undertake in the capital lens process is to create a comprehensive profile of the business and the industry, and match it with an appropriate capital markets strategy and capital structure profile. That profile should include the capital instruments, markets, and partners that will power the company's long-term business plan most effectively.

In 2014, a small family-owned company reached a difficult point with its lenders. The company had repeatedly violated covenants of its bank loan, owing to unrealistic expectations and business changes. This put its leaders in a situation where operating flexibility was limited, capital was constrained, and the relationship with their long-time lender began to sour. They needed a fresh perspective and sought an outside view of the situation.

The capital structure consisted of numerous one-off debt instruments from different providers, none of whom talked to each other, and each seemed to care only about what fell within its purview. Though the company had a top-down strategic vision and operating plan, none of the capital providers had bought into the plan. They either didn't know about it or, for their own reasons, had no incentive to support it. Managers were spending too much time dealing with lender requests, amendments, and legal documents, and not enough time tending to the business. Existing lenders wouldn't provide fresh capital. Ultimately, it became obvious that the company's capital structure was inhibiting growth rather than enabling it.

A review through the capital lens of the business and the owners' objectives yielded critical insights: the business was asset-heavy, the company planned to be acquisitive, the industry was hypercompetitive, and owners expected a continuation of dividends. Management's financing objectives were to reduce its capital costs, extend tenor (the amount of time left to repay a loan), and gain more flexibility and liquidity. They matched these key findings with the defining characteristics of available capital instruments, markets, and providers. Managers began to make out what the optimal capital structure should be, and how to convince stakeholders of the soundness of their new plan.

First, the asset-heavy nature of the business required a financing vehicle like an asset-based loan (ABL), which relied predominantly on asset values. Second, asset-based financing also provided more operational flexibility for making acquisitions, besting the competition, and paying dividends. The ABL had a lower cost of capital than other instruments because it had strict controls on borrowing levels, and relied more heavily on repayment from asset liquidation than repayment from operational cash.

Finally, with assets available to back an ABL, the company was able to increase liquidity by 30% and extend tenor by more than three years. Ultimately, the company placed its four disparate loan facilities inside a single ABL that satisfied the company's operational, strategic, and financing objectives. Managers found unified support among their new lending group and significantly reduced managerial time spent on lender requests and documentation. The company, with sufficient capital available to fulfill its strategic objectives, soon began to refocus on growing the business. At last, rather than holding the business back, the capital structure was fueling the business.

Management's journey to assess and redefine its capital structure was not easy. Given the financial stress on the business, managers had no choice but to proactively address their capital structure. Corporate executives can do themselves a big favor by taking on these issues long before being forced to do so. If they cannot fully optimize in the short term, then they should at least take steps to restructure over time. Figure 7.1 provides an overall framework for the capital lens, the

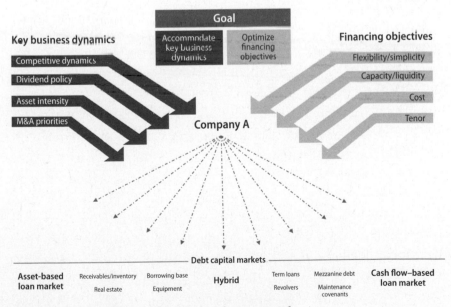

Figure 7.1   The capital lens framework

nexus where business dynamics and financing objectives converge and point to a suitable capital structure.

Assess strategic financing alternatives

The next exercise in the capital lens process is to determine both short- and long-term business needs. This can be accomplished by a thorough review of the following areas on the way to developing an implementation plan.

Strategic, financial, legal, and tax priorities

As we've discussed throughout the book, Capital Agenda decisions require you to synthesize and balance many, sometimes competing, priorities:

- *Business strategy and financial considerations.* These form the foundation of capital structure analysis because the choice of capital structure can substantially help or hinder your strategy and Capital Agenda. Management should consider both the short term and the long term by asking the following questions:
    1. Are we pursuing organic or acquisitive growth?
    2. What are the competitive dynamics within the industry, and how do we expect them to evolve?
    3. How volatile are manufacturing inputs?
    4. What capital is required to fund construction of a new plant, broaden a product line, or expand into a new geography?
    5. How much interest rate fluctuation can we absorb?
    6. What is the advantage to owning versus leasing business assets?
    7. Will asset sales become important in the future?
    8. Do shareholders expect dividend distributions or share repurchases today or in the near future?
    9. What are the long-term goals of the owners/shareholders (particularly relevant for privately owned companies)?

- *Legal structure.* Management must evaluate the company's legal structure and regulatory environment in terms of transparency in public reporting, minimum capital requirements, legal jurisdictions of operations, and any legal or regulatory threats.
- *Tax structure and strategy.* Management must also review the tax implications of any capital decisions in terms of location of operations and the repatriation of foreign earnings, organizational structure and type, potential timing of transactions, and possible deductions of interest expense.

Key considerations and trade-offs associated with potential financing options

After identifying business strategy, financial, legal, and tax priorities, managers should define their financing objectives as they relate to business needs. This involves analyzing, both quantitatively and qualitatively, the various capital structure options available relative to these objectives. Each option comes with a unique set of pros and cons.

There are many trade-offs of various capital instruments, but the four key areas are flexibility, liquidity, tenor, and cost.

1. *Flexibility/simplicity.* At its highest level, there is a trade-off between flexibility and cost of capital. Generally, if capital gives a company greater flexibility and its provider takes on more risk, then it will demand higher returns. Management should evaluate the level of flexibility required to execute business strategy. For example, acquisitive growth generally requires more flexibility. Companies that experience earnings volatility because of cyclicality or seasonality may also require flexibility, especially in covenants. Companies that operate with predictable cash flow may give up flexibility for lower cost of capital.
2. *Liquidity/capacity.* Management should also consider the degree of liquidity required for both short- and long-term objectives. They should evaluate the drivers of the company's liquidity needs (seasonality, opportunism) and the business (by unit and

geography) that needs it. A company with substantial international operations must also consider cross-border capital flows and its ability to move cash to units that need it.

3. *Tenor.* Once management has reviewed the nature of its investments and expected cash flows, they should evaluate the tenor of their capital structure—that is, the length of time until the company must repay a loan or until a debt contract expires. For example, a short-term financing structure could disrupt a long-term expansion plan. Conversely, a company with only short-term liquidity needs may avoid accessing longer-term capital with terms that prohibit or penalize early repayment. Tenor can also affect the cost of capital.

4. *Cost.* Many companies focus on cost of capital at the expense of flexibility, liquidity, and tenor. Cost of capital is effectively a function of risk, which is managed through flexibility and control. Managers must consider the company's business strategy and investment opportunities to determine how much debt service it can sustain, and then prioritize cost of capital relative to other objectives.

Review financing options and select a structure

Companies often have access to a variety of financing options, ranging from secured debt instruments to unsecured debt instruments and to hybrid and equity instruments (see Figure 7.2). Once managers identify their core financing objectives, the relative advantages and disadvantages of these various instruments are easier to rank and evaluate. In many cases, multiple structures meet both business and financing objectives. Managers should assess current market conditions (that is, the ability to execute) and weigh the attributes of alternative financing structures before making a final selection.

In many cases, companies are reactive when it comes to financing and capital structure. Instead of employing a methodical approach as previously outlined, they might react to ideas or pitches from managers,

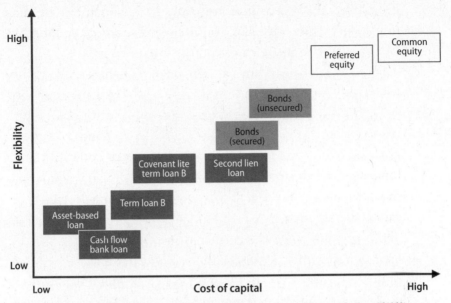

Figure 7.2   Instruments for different ranges of flexibility and cost of capital

board members, capital providers, or other advisors. This can lead to sub-optimal outcomes. Managers who have proactively analyzed, discussed, and agreed upon their key business dynamics and financing objectives are better positioned to act on their goals and approach financing providers and the capital markets with a well-vetted capital plan.

Execute on the implementation plan

Once management has chosen an optimal structure, they must develop a plan for realizing it. Companies should take as much care ensuring a smooth execution as they did with selecting the right structure. Executing this plan effectively is critical to accommodating those business dynamics and optimizing those original financial objectives. Management can take four actions to improve execution:

1. *Conduct a formal competitive financing process.* Sometimes management is reluctant to submit existing capital providers to a

formal, competitive process. But if done correctly, warm relationships can be maintained while the company benefits from the natural positive effects that a competitive process can produce. Not only can a formal competition enhance a company's information flow and negotiating leverage, but it can also help to recalibrate existing capital-provider relationships and cultivate new ones. Once managers decide to conduct a competitive process, they need to identify potential capital providers according to their financing needs, distribute a comprehensive request for proposal (RFP), and conduct in-person meetings.

2. *Pick financing partners wisely*. Today's capital markets include many highly capable financing institutions. Managers should keep in mind that their strongest relationships today may not be the strongest partners to execute the desired capital structure. During the selection process, managers should seek objective, outside views of the core competencies of each prospective partner. This can be accomplished by seeking the opinions of bankers, colleagues at other companies, advisors, and contacts at industry associations. The financing source must be able to do what management is asking it to—not just now but throughout the tenor of the capital and potentially beyond. Ideally, financing partners will have the capabilities for the job and will be a cultural fit with the company. Particularly for middle-market companies with limited in-house resources, partners should also have a good mix of balance-sheet capital, capital markets and M&A advice, and ancillary products and services like derivatives, trading, and cash management.

3. *Maintain options*. Before choosing a financing provider, and when a company is negotiating key terms of the deal, management should negotiate a detailed term sheet up front with multiple financing providers. Once the company chooses a provider, that provider has little motivation to provide flexibility, so the company will lose leverage and options in the negotiation. This approach will also reduce the risk of overlooking terms (particularly those that

limit flexibility) that end up reducing flexibility or worsening the economics of the deal in later stages of negotiation or documentation. During execution, having an alternate financing path or structure can help mitigate negative market movements. Such options might take the form of an alternate financial instrument, a separate market or marketing process, or slight changes in structure or terms. Changing course in the middle of a transaction rarely bodes well for the issuer of the financing. Managers should insist on analyzing and discussing these changes and should prepare to effect such changes before launch.

4. *Stay abreast of the market.* Market conditions can change daily, and some markets are more volatile than others. Managers need accurate market information for sound decision making, whether it relates to prices, the deal pipeline, capital flows, or specific execution details on precedent transactions. Most companies get their market information from the capital providers that call on them. Managers should seek multiple perspectives to make sure they have a multidimensional view.

Achieving capital structure flexibility and efficiency

A company's capital structure, financing strategy, and plan for effective implementation can have a substantial effect on the execution of business strategy and on the ultimate success of the company. Time invested to identify and obtain the right capital structure can pay dividends later by reducing the likelihood that management will have to continually wrestle with the financing challenges of a suboptimal structure.

Not every business executive will have an opportunity to devise a capital structure to accompany a record US$25 billion investment as did Henry Kravis, but many are charged with a similar task of optimizing capital structure to improve their business. Approaching the task in a thorough and comprehensive way will allow managers and shareholders to benefit from a durable capital structure that serves as a powerful facilitator of the business's goals and objectives.

8 | How well does working capital management contribute to cash flow and earnings?

Sven Braun and Steve Payne

If cash is king, why do so few companies take proper care of it? One of our recent studies used peer-to-peer performance comparison as a proxy, and found that more than US$1 trillion is tied up in excess working capital in companies across the globe. Why is all this unproductive cash just sitting around, waiting to be claimed by someone who knows where to look?

Sometimes companies focus too much on the income statement (revenue, profitability, and earnings), while overlooking key aspects of the balance sheet. Specifically, they forget about the importance of executing on the policies and processes that optimize the level of working capital required to support their business. This is exactly what happened when a major pharmaceutical company carved out a subsidiary in an attempt to focus on its core business. Being cash-rich, the parent company historically did not have a strong focus on working capital. In contrast, the private equity house that bought the subsidiary focused on working capital to drive value creation, generate free cash to pay down debt, and improve the company's operations.

Within six months of focusing on the incentives, policies, and processes that drive and influence working capital, around US$100 million in cash was liberated. If the parent had done this work prior to the carve-out, the sale might have been valued at a higher multiple and the parent would have benefited from retaining the additional cash. Instead, this cash went to the buyer. In our experience, buyers rarely compensate sellers in full for the value of their excess working capital. It's a value-creation gift happily accepted.

Why working capital matters

Useful discussions around working capital can get extremely technical, and the sheer number of acronyms rivals what one might find in a military campaign plan. (That's why we have a glossary.) Though the issues may be more complex than one might imagine, the concept of working capital as a value driver is really very simple. It revolves around deeply understanding opportunities by measuring the right things, and then seizing those opportunities to improve key processes.

It is puzzling why many companies focus purely on sales and profit and do not put the proper emphasis on cash flow. After all, it's common to see companies that generate a profit but become stressed or distressed due to insufficient cash flow. This happens when managers miss opportunities because they treat working capital as a consequence of their business and measure it reactively, using performance metrics defined by accounting schools decades ago. Working capital performance is a window into how effective a company is at the operational execution of its strategy. It should not be about playing quarter-or year-end games and leveraging financial tools to project a cosmetic level of results in order to look good to analysts and shareholders. The best performance metrics not only are insightful, but they also reinforce good habits.

Leaders are in the best position to seize opportunities when they value the advantages of optimizing working capital, internalize the right mindset, and follow the process. These opportunities can liberate millions—and sometimes even billions—of dollars that are trapped, and can be used to fund the investments required to achieve strategic imperatives. What are some of these strategic imperatives?

- Cash liberated from working capital is the cheapest source of liquidity and can be used to fund acquisitions, repay debt, return cash to shareholders, or pay for the implementation of an enterprise-wide technology system.
- Shareholder activism is on the rise, and one of the most cited areas of value creation is increased cash flow. Optimizing working capital will help ward off activist shareholders when they see one of the value wells of opportunity is dry.
- Most industries are cyclical, and in the downstroke of a cycle, it's preferable to be one of the companies with strong cash flow. That way, when analysts do their rankings and call out the poorly performing companies, they're referring to someone else. This can help to protect your stock price and protect the brand from negative news.
- Transactions are opportunities to reset cash flow performance. For example, once an acquisition has been completed, implementing leading practices between the parent and the new asset can lift the operational performance of the whole and generate even more cash and value.

Stress test your working capital proficiency

Even with the substantial benefits of optimizing working capital, it's an unfortunate reality that most companies have not done so.

Some companies are cash-rich, including many technology and life sciences companies. These firms may recognize the theoretical benefit of optimizing every facet of their business, but they have more urgent priorities. Freeing up something they already have a great deal of is usually not a main concern. That is, until the tides turn.

Consider how the oil and gas sector often has very strong cash flow and profitability when oil prices are high. Executives have little interest in optimizing their working capital processes. Then, when the price per barrel plummets, cash flows dry up quickly. The high fixed-cost structures result in stress, distress, and bankruptcy.

Sometimes, executives are just not aware of the potential "free" cash tied up in their inventory, payables, and receivables. It is often the case that even if they are aware, they don't know how to fully unlock this value. The reason is that finance is typically accountable for working capital, but sales and operations own the processes that need to be fixed.

Let's assume you would like to assess how much you could realize from improving your approach to working capital. Here is a series of questions that provide you with an initial understanding of how well your organization owns key elements of working capital management.

Your working capital baseline

1. Do you really know the cash flow required to fund operations?
2. Based on your supply base, supply chain, and customer base, do you know what the optimal level of working capital is?
3. Are you comfortable enough with the stability of your operations to actually reduce cash or liquidity levels to this baseline?

Responsibilities

4. Do you provide incentives to your business leaders to achieve forecasted cash flow targets?
5. Are your business leaders held accountable for working capital levels?
6. Do you hold people accountable for achieving targets annually, quarterly, monthly, or even weekly?

Accounts receivable

7. Do you think days sales outstanding (DSO) is an insightful metric?
8. Do you know the gap between weighted average terms (WAT) and days to collect?
9. Do you know what triggers the cycle of your customers to start their payment processes (e.g. receipt of goods/services, receipt of invoice, or date of invoice)?
10. Do your customers typically take every early or prompt payment discount but still pay late?
11. Do you factor or securitize accounts receivable (AR) even when you do not need to, or when you can't access the cash?

Accounts payable

12. Have you changed your payment terms in the past five years?
13. Are your payment term targets differentiated by spend category?
14. When negotiating price and terms with major suppliers, do you review their DSOs?
15. Do you pay invoices early, even without the inducement of discounts?

Inventory

16. Have you adjusted your inventory target days in the past six months to align with your desired customer-service goals?
17. Do you need to make goods to reduce or achieve your target cost per unit?
18. Do you have excess capacity that you could use to make smaller batches?
19. Do you have too many stock keeping units (SKUs)?
20. Have past attempts to reduce the number of SKUs met your objectives?

21. Do you know how much inventory you've written off across the enterprise in the past five years?
22. Do you know specifically why you've written off inventory? (Because it expired, or you're making the wrong products, etc.)

Answering these questions should stimulate more thought and have you exploring options, even for those that were positive.

In our experience, companies that are new to the journey of improving and maintaining good working capital will not know the answers to more than half of these questions. If that describes you, it may be good news in the sense that you have the potential to make substantial improvements. The very act of tracking this information will get you started in the right direction.

Companies often start with the best intentions, but they learn that plenty of things that should be done to sustainably reduce working capital requirements are counterintuitive. For example, a company was having issues with high levels of unbilled and aged AR. Its solution was to speed the issuance of invoices. Though unbilled levels dropped, the overall size of the issue got worse as the aged receivables grew exponentially. The root cause was the poor quality of the invoices that resulted in excessive disputes with customers. This consumed the collections function, which slowed cash collection even more.

If you are serious about optimizing your working capital and were not able to get answers to some of the questions, then we recommend that you make finding the answers your first order of business. These are fundamental and important areas for anyone driving a business to know well, yet few executives do.

Are you using outdated metrics?

The next step is to make sure you're measuring the right things. Unfortunately, the working capital metrics most companies use to help steer their business are not serving them the way they should.

We're talking about three very common metrics: DSO, days payables outstanding (DPO), and days inventory outstanding (DIO). These metrics are *somewhat* useful if you want to compare similar business units within your company to each other, or compare your current performance to history. It is also important to note that companies should be flexible enough to calculate certain metrics if there are specific reasons to do so. For example, DSO, DPO, and DIO are the metrics that analysts will want to review, because that is all they get access to from the outside. But for audiences on the inside, DSO is almost never the right metric.

Companies often use these metrics to compare performance against peers. However, doing this is problematic because there are many different working capital elements you cannot see that could distort the results, such as:

- Customer base, geographic footprint, and business model can have a big effect on DSO. Additionally, DSO measures the AR balance at only a specific point in time, so it allows for late payments over a long duration in which the measure is not taken.
- Accounting rules are interpreted differently, and decisions such as reporting value-added tax (VAT) payables as part of accounts payable (AP) versus extracting them can have large effects on DPO as an outside-in benchmark. The inverse effect happens on VAT receivables and AR.
- The level of vertical integration affects DIO. Specifically, vertically integrated companies will be penalized on DIO while sometimes showing higher profitability.

Even if you are truly measuring apples to apples, relative outperformance takes you only so far. If activists think you could do even better in an absolute sense, you could soon be subject to their critique.

To provide a more specific example for AR management, consider the following: DSO does not tell you how your performance compares to the weighted terms of your outstanding invoices. Not only is this metric unable to measure your performance against your own terms, using it to compare to your peers—assuming you select the right ones—is limited by your not knowing their terms. As a result, using DSO does not allow you to assess the full extent of the improvement opportunity.

Many companies also need to elevate their operational AR metrics to the next level. One old-school measure is aged receivables. Companies will produce an aging report at the end of the month and show the percentage current, and then the percentages of the aged balances in various time-based buckets (e.g. 30–45 and 45–60 days). Today, big data analytics allow us to get more insightful metrics. One example of the weakness of the aged report is that it misses opportunities to reduce late payments *within* the month. A customer could pay 20+ days late, take an early/prompt payment discount, and fly under the radar, yet in some cases be deemed a good customer because the customer paid within the month.

This is where WAT and weighted average days to collect (WADC) are different. WAT measures the time the customer is entitled to hold back payment as defined by the credit terms, and weighs it by the invoice amount, and WADC measures the duration it took you to collect for each invoice. When taken together, these metrics show the real gap between the baseline of entitlement and current performance. Even more, they allow you to segment the customer base on a weighted transactional level as well as predict customer behavior. Similar to the example used earlier, it is important to understand the "why" in the performance gap—what part is self-inflicted and what part is driven by customer behavior or circumstance. Then you can build improvement actions into the collections strategy for each customer segment.

Years ago, when computing power was relatively rare and expensive, it was not feasible to have calculations based on actual transaction data. Now it is.

The WAT and WADC metrics are transaction-based. They allow you to answer questions such as: "Based on the terms that we have agreed to with all of our customers, how long should it take us to collect?"

Putting modern analytics into practice

Now that we have clarified the importance of establishing the right metrics, we need to make sure we can use them. Transaction-based metrics enable you to fully understand your cash entitlement from trade and nontrade working capital. They enable you to own your cash flow in a way that maximizes the benefits from your operations.

When you know your minimal AR balance, based on your weighted average collection terms, you can use this information to define targets for your collections organization. This will help improve performance because the targets are based on reality. Furthermore, you can identify how customers pay and, based on the size of the customer's portfolio, prioritize where and how to focus on collections improvement. Not all customers are created equal when it comes to collections, and different strategies should be built based on where they fit into a customer stratification matrix. The result of shifting from high-level to transactional metrics is actionable insight and a real understanding of your potential cash flow baseline.

Once you understand your baseline, you can better define your financial planning around cash flow, and assess trade-offs among working capital changes. For example, you might sell more into international markets where payment terms are typically longer, requiring more working capital than many domestic markets.

The psychology is harder than the math

Even though this is a chapter about the decidedly nonemotional subject of managing working capital, it's important to step back at this point to consider psychology and persuasion.

Why? Because implementing a working capital improvement program is a change-management process as much as it is about implementing leading policies, processes, and metrics. To ensure sustainability, it is important to win people's minds with insights into what they can be doing differently, but also to win their hearts by making sure they understand why change is needed.

A company may have strong natural cash flow due to high margins, and it may never have had to worry about liquidity. As a result, it may have a culture of driving sales through giving away longer payment terms—something that's hard to rein in without a costly incentive when sales slow in a down cycle. Another undisciplined practice is to offer customers every product in every color to avoid missing any sales of high-margin products. The resulting excess inventory introduces a complexity that leads to write-offs, especially when the company lacks sophisticated inventory management experience to fulfill its customer-service goals.

Another example of poor execution with the best of intentions happens when an executive decides her company has too much inventory and issues a mandate to reduce it. The organization reduces inventory levels, but then starts to be late fulfilling customer orders and misses sales. The next mandate is to improve customer-service levels, which is done by increasing inventory. The fundamental misunderstanding is that inventory results from a process that is supported by policies. To reduce inventories, one has to make changes to the policies and processes that result in operational improvements and allow inventory to be reduced while maintaining customer-service levels. Lowering inventory without changes to key processes is forcing a level of inventory beyond the existing operational capability of the supply chain; in doing so, the company falls short of its customer-service goals.

This is both a cultural and technical challenge, and you need to address both. When doing so, it's best to put the focus on the measurements and processes, and not on the people involved.

Harry Truman said: "It is amazing what you can accomplish if you do not care who gets the credit." To the extent that you can make others the heroes for optimizing working capital, they may become the biggest proponents of the initiative.

Important note: You can talk all you want about optimizing working capital, but if people's compensation is not tied to doing so, you're unlikely to get the buy-in you need. Here is what we recommend for tying compensation to working capital optimization: the profit-and-loss (P&L) statement has to be a focus but the ultimate priority should be long-term value creation. As such, managers should be incentivized primarily on cash flow, and secondarily on profit.

Next steps in the optimization journey

Of course, the full optimization of working capital for any company will involve many detailed steps and customizations. Each journey will be different based on the urgency of cash need, operating model, culture, and many other elements.

From our experience, the most successful journeys start with knowing where you are and where you want to go, and then deciding how you want to get there. The first phase should identify the improvement opportunities and, most important, quantify them so an effective prioritization can take place. For example, the value of a DSO improvement of 30 days in one country may not deliver as much cash as a four-day improvement in another.

A working capital journey should be about executing the plan, and this is where both the technical and cultural changes are made. It is important to get some quick wins early, because nothing encourages enthusiasm as much as success. Here are some factors that can help to maximize your results:

- *Executive sponsorship*. Unless working capital optimization is seen as a priority by the C-suite, the results often will be limited and unsustainable.
- *Effective governance*. These programs are complex and involve many functions that affect and influence working capital; they must be in sync. There are trade-off decisions to be made and there will be times when different functions sit on opposing sides of the decision. An effective and ongoing plan will need leadership.

- *Cascading metrics*. Establish the appropriate, consistent metrics that reflect the hierarchy of needs across the company. Expect to deliver appropriate metrics to different users: the CEO and CFO must be able to communicate with the board, with shareholders, and with analysts. At the same time, the person calling customers to collect invoices for goods or services must have useful metrics for that function.
- *Incentives*. Consider tying a sufficient amount of variable compensation to attaining cash flow and working capital objectives. This approach establishes a level of seriousness to the priorities. A mandate for a strategic priority that does not affect compensation will never meet its full potential.
- *Change management*. Establish a forum for those making the changes to present their actions and results to the executive sponsor. This will help ensure that managers on the front lines of driving the change are well versed in the details and working to ensure sustainability. They will then be seen as solid per-formers by those who affect future careers and compensation.

9

Is tax a full partner in building resilience and driving value?

Bridget Walsh and Erica Lawee

In a recent acquisition, a multinational company (MNC) felt the pain of involving tax expertise too late in the deal process. Their deal teams submitted a nonbinding offer without doing proper tax due diligence. The offer was at the top end of the bid prices received, and the company was selected as a preferred bidder. Two days prior to submitting the binding offer, the tax teams were brought in and discovered the target used a tax structure for its international business that was incompatible with the company's structure, and that materially decreased the deal's internal rate of return (IRR). The final offer was submitted with a clause that the company refused to acquire an interest in the international business, given the way it was structured. Consequently, they were removed from the auction process. Not only did this create tension with the target, but it also created friction between the tax department and the deal team, which lost what had otherwise appeared to be a lucrative deal.

Key tax issues affecting business today

Across the global corporate landscape, tax is an increasingly important business issue in deal making and capital allocation decisions. Tax itself is becoming a disruptive factor, with domestic and international tax reforms, and rising international political and media interest in MNC tax affairs. Tax should move from the back office to the boardroom once senior executives begin to understand its far-reaching implications for the Capital Agenda—from financial, reputational, and strategic perspectives.

Despite accelerating change and growing complexity, the tax function's challenges remain the same: to deliver value, manage costs, and mitigate risk.

EY has identified three key issues that will drive tax risks and opportunities in the near term and beyond:

1. The pace of legislative change
2. Taxation of the digital economy
3. A heightened tax-controversy environment

The pace of legislative change

Legislative tax reforms and technological advances allow for information transfers among states, provinces, government agencies, and increasingly global tax authorities from different countries. This has resulted in major changes in tax policy, as countries around the world begin to adopt new tax laws or dramatically change the way they interpret existing laws, including tax treaties, for a digitalized and globalized economy.

Base erosion and profit shifting initiative: Transforming cross-border transactions

A fundamental way in which tax is affecting deals is the Organisation for Economic Co-operation and Development (OECD)'s base erosion and profit shifting (BEPS) project, which was initiated in 2013 by the G20 and OECD countries. It aims to address perceived international tax avoidance stemming from mismatches among the domestic tax regimes of different countries.

Three main objectives guide BEPS's implementation:

1. Countries' tax laws should be internationally coherent and not leave any income inappropriately untaxed or double-taxed.
2. Profits should be taxed where value is created.
3. Tax authorities should have insight into the global operations of taxpayers and be able to share relevant tax information with each other.

New, subjective rules are driving more tax disputes, a lack of access to cross-border treaty relief (such as withholding taxes on dividends, interest, and royalties), and potentially higher future financing costs, among other things. Specifically, BEPS includes changes designed to:

- Limit interest deductions.
- Eliminate the benefits of hybrid financing arrangements.
- Lower the permanent establishment standards for taxable presence in a country.
- Place new restrictions on access to benefits of tax treaties.
- Provide transfer pricing guidelines that better align the taxation of profits with economic activities.
- Require new country-by-country reporting.

BEPS-related tax law changes may effectively increase the cost of capital for many companies and private equity funds. For many taxpayers, restrictions on interest deductibility, use of hybrid instruments, and access to tax treaties have reduced the related tax shield, materially affecting the cost of debt financing. This new BEPS environment makes it essential to realign structure and operational transfer pricing to maximize transaction value.

BEPS's approach to taxing profits where value is created means that tax planning must be fully integrated with operational decisions. It is critical for the business and tax functions to work together to review current business models and supply chains, and evaluate where essential changes need to be made.

US Tax Cuts and Jobs Act

In December 2017, the United States enacted the most sweeping overhaul of its tax system in more than three decades, which resulted in lowering the corporate tax rate, broadening the base, and moving the United States to a quasi-territorial tax system. The US Tax Cuts and Jobs Act (US TCJA) affects a range of corporations and private equity stakeholders, including those headquartered in the United States and abroad. For many non-US corporations, the United States is their biggest market and their largest tax burden.

Like BEPS, the US TCJA's implications extend far beyond the tax department to functions including operations, compensation and benefits, financing, and treasury. For example, restrictions on interest deductibility result in changes in tax strategy and capital structure, especially when leverage has been one way that foreign multinationals addressed the United States' relatively high tax expense.

Company executives also need to consider scenarios in which other governments adjust their tax regimes in order to respond to the United States' more competitive environment. Further rate reductions outside the United States, increased tax incentives, and retaliatory trade measures are all possibilities you should consider when stress testing investment evaluations.

What this means for your company

The current changes occurring in the global tax landscape are forcing adaptation not only in tax planning and compliance processes, but also in how enterprises conduct their core businesses. Companies must consider a broad range of issues as they refresh their strategies, design and adapt business models, conduct due diligence, and structure and price transactions:

- Effective tax rate consequences
- Intellectual property strategy
- Supply chain and operating model configuration
- Legal entity structure
- Information technology needs
- Relationships with tax policy makers and administrators
- Availability of tax incentives for innovation
- Cash repatriation

Board directors, senior executives, and tax directors not only need to consider historical tax exposures, but also must ensure that their current tax structures remain fit for purpose.

Taxing the digital economy

Today, nearly every company has a digital presence and derives value from data. As companies continue down the digital path, there will be far-reaching effects across organizations in shifting the value chain, the manner of customer interaction, use of data, and the location of people and physical assets.

The digital economy also affects the BEPS initiative, which seeks to tax profits in the countries where the company has a permanent establishment. Important criteria include where it undertakes value-generating activities, where major operating decisions are made, and where important assets and risks are controlled.

Historically, the tax system has been based on the physical manufacture and supply of goods and provision of services. In digital businesses, however, there may be limited or no physical presence in the country where consumer transactions take place.

Consider online retailers using platforms to connect buyers and sellers, social media networks that rely on advertising revenues, and subscription-based models. Countries have varying ideas about how value is created in digital business models and how that value should be taxed.

Tax authorities around the world are beginning to adapt to the digital economy. These changes reflect governments' attempts to catch up with new cross-border business models employing cutting-edge technologies. However, in practice, these new laws are often inconsistent and create more risks, higher compliance burdens, and greater levels of planning uncertainty.

Paying the right amount of tax in a country can be a complex endeavor, even when the intentions are to maintain the best possible compliance. As technology and the digital economy drive new, complex digital tax laws around the world, executives must work closely with their tax teams to stay abreast of this changing environment, focusing on these questions in particular:

- What are the additional tax risks?
- How does my digital strategy affect my effective tax rate?
- Does my transfer pricing strategy need to change?
- Is my tax structure still fit for purpose?
- Does my digital strategy create new permanent establishments that could be subject to additional taxation?

A heightened tax controversy environment

Governments challenge each other, as well as companies, to get what they see as their fair share of taxable revenue.

At its most basic, tax controversy is a dispute between a taxpayer and a tax authority. The potential for controversy has reached new heights with international tax reforms, information sharing among tax authorities, digitalization, and the media spotlight on tax, as well as subsequent political reactions. As a result, there has been a substantial increase in the number and size of tax audits, assessments, and disputes with revenue authorities worldwide.

Increased scrutiny and litigation by tax authorities also generate much greater visibility for the tax department at the board level. Following significant public scrutiny and media attention around whether certain high-profile multinationals were paying their fair share of taxes, tax affairs are increasingly linked to corporate reputation. Fully 70% of large businesses responding to EY's recent Tax Risk and Controversy Survey indicated they are concerned about media coverage, and 60% of survey respondents said they think tax disputes will increase.

Controversial actions can extend beyond the financial risks of additional taxes, interest, penalties, legal fees, or potential share-price erosion. Disputes with tax authorities can create a drain on senior management focus and business confidence, as well as reputational damage in the eyes of consumers and other stakeholders. It is vital that the tax function works alongside the board and the C-suite to develop a clear tax policy framework. It must explain the company's approach to tax planning, to ensure its tax obligations are met from an operating and risk-management perspective.

Examples of the increasingly difficult tax controversy environment include the European Commission investigations of whether certain agreements between companies and tax authorities (such as advance tax rulings and advance pricing agreements for transfer pricing) may constitute unlawful state aid. In the absence of more effective dispute resolution mechanisms, particularly across borders, business leaders need to understand the potential for challenges in every relevant jurisdiction.

In some companies with a high level of ongoing tax controversy, there may be a perception at the board level that transactions or planning approaches carry greater risk in today's era of aggressive tax administration than ever before. Whether or not a company is involved in a tax dispute or tax-related reputational risk issue, it is here that the tax function takes a deeper role in helping shape corporate strategy.

The surge of tax controversy—heightened rules, regulations, interagency cooperation and communication—is placing a heavy burden on companies around the world. In response, executives should be asking themselves three questions related to tax planning:

1. Is my approach legally effective, and do the benefits outweigh the costs of execution and defense?
2. Is my approach aligned with the intent and purpose of the law?
3. Can I justify the outcome in a public forum?

Tax in the Capital Agenda

International tax reforms, digitalization, and a heightened controversy environment have transformed the global tax landscape and contributed to the elevated role of tax on the boardroom agenda. Planning for any restructuring, realignment, or transaction in a single country or across borders requires factoring in an ever-broader range of tax-related issues—from effective tax rate and legal entity structures to supply chain and operating models; from intellectual property strategy to information technology needs; and from treasury function to exit strategy.

Stress test your overall tax function involvement

We recommend that you stress test the current priority you attach to your tax function by answering the following questions:

- Have you had situations where the tax effects of a transaction or other activity had to be calculated in a rushed fashion, when you could have brought in the tax advisory team earlier?
- In recent deals, has lack of preparation in dealing with tax risks been a source of value erosion?
- Are you lacking a globally coordinated approach for tax risk and controversy?

■ Have any of your tax positions been challenged—formally or informally—and, if so, did you have a robust, preexisting rationale to support your positions?

If you answered "Yes" to any of these questions, then we recommend that you consider getting your tax advisors involved sooner, and at a higher level of your organization.

Let's next look at specific areas across your Capital Agenda where tax plays an important role.

Every transaction has unique tax implications

Tax has always been an important consideration in transactions. However, as average deal sizes have increased, so too has the complexity of the deals, often with more international and cross-border issues—and potentially, more material tax costs.

Specifically, the changing tax environment will affect transactions in the following ways:

■ *Due diligence.* Tax due diligence plays a critical role, requiring assessment of not only historical tax exposures, but also the effects of changing tax legislation on the target's tax position and investment model in the future. Moreover, this environment of heightened tax enforcement and controversy demands deeper questions about the target's approach to managing tax controversy, and new ways of managing tax risk, including additional clauses in purchase agreements and tax-specific indemnity insurance. Due diligence also informs the view of tax items to be included in the deal pricing balance sheet.

■ *Potential valuation effects.* Tax is increasingly affecting the pricing of deals, whether it be from issues identified in due diligence or modeling the effect of tax law changes. Finance costs are central to valuation and transaction pricing, with deal pricing and valuations sensitive to interest deductions for tax purposes and their effect on after-tax cash flows. US- and BEPS-related tax law changes resulting in restrictions on interest deductibility, use of hybrid instruments, and access to tax treaties may reduce the related tax shield and increase the cost of capital for many multinationals and PE funds. This may be even more material on long-term investments with high levels of debt capacity (e.g. infrastructure), where the effect on overall value of interest deductions may be significant.

- *Transaction structuring considerations.* Tax is often integral to the structure of a deal. Engaging with tax advisors up front to identify structural alternatives can translate to a negotiating advantage and help maximize transaction value. Deal structures and sources of financing need to be carefully considered to ensure that deductibility of interest is achieved and funds can be efficiently repatriated with minimal tax leakage. New tax laws will drive an increase in bespoke tax structuring. In addition, both reputational risk and challenges by tax authorities will need to be carefully considered in how the deal is structured.

- *Postdeal integration and maintenance.* Tax advisors need to work alongside the deal team and businesspeople to realize the investment thesis to ensure successful implementation of the tax plan in conjunction with commercial and legal strategies. Initiatives to improve operating model efficiency, including supply-chain optimization and IP rationalization, need to be considered within the lens of BEPS and other tax reforms' increasing scrutiny of where value is created. Following an integration, postdeal reporting and compliance capabilities will need to be assessed to meet the complex and demanding new disclosure requirements.

Divestments

EY's recent Global Capital Confidence Barometer survey found that when evaluating a business portfolio, it is critical that the tax team be actively engaged with the broader business to understand the overall strategy and to help ensure that any divestment strategy balances tax implications with commercial and operational drivers.[1]

Our recent Global Corporate Divestment Study surveyed 900 senior corporate executives who had divested in the past three years. The data show that those who clearly described tax assets to purchasers were better able to drive value. Considering tax early in the process enables companies to more accurately identify tax implications of the divestment upfront, and to design flexibility into their sales structures and deal negotiations.[2]

Just how much value can tax add to a divestment? We hosted a tax workshop with a UK-headquartered company that was considering divesting a division that was doing business in 12 countries. During the workshop we identified that the tax cost on exit could be significantly reduced with a presale reorganization. Given this proactive analysis, there was time to work though the steps and be in a position to present the reorganized structure to the purchaser. As part of its planning, the company consulted with employees, reviewed key contracts for the ability to assign, and tested financial systems to reflect separation. Without the up-front consideration, the operational challenges would have meant the reorganization could not have been undertaken, leaving 10% of the sale proceeds on the table.

Restructuring

Tax also plays a pivotal role in the restructuring of companies we discuss in Chapter 14. A turnaround and restructuring plan may involve reducing operating costs, modifying debt agreements, reorganizing the corporate structure, or selling assets. No matter which alternatives the company or its creditors choose, proactive tax planning will help avoid unexpected tax consequences and preserve value for stakeholders.

The restructuring and tax teams should work with creditors to develop reorganization plans that preserve valuable tax assets such as net operating loss carryforwards and depreciable asset basis. They can consider strategies to release cash, monetize tax attributes, and reduce tax. Understanding the tax implications of alternative corporate and financing structures from both debtor and creditor perspectives leads to improved negotiations and more cost-effective agreements.

Turning tax uncertainty into opportunity across the Capital Agenda

Legislative trends, digitalization, and rising controversy add new layers of complexity to executive decision making. CEOs and CFOs who treat tax planning as an essential discipline in their Capital Agenda are best positioned to leverage tax assets as a competitive advantage, and avoid unnecessary risks. As companies look to thrive in a technologically disrupted world by designing new business models, tax considerations will need to be front and center.

Notes

1. EY Global Capital Confidence Barometer is a regular survey of senior executives from large companies around the world, conducted by Euromoney Institutional Investor Thought Leadership.
2. EY Global Corporate Divestment Study 2018, based on responses of 900 global corporate executives, offers statistical analysis of divestment priorities and reported performance on sale price of their most recent divestment.

10

Are strategy, finance, and operations integrated for optimal value creation?

Sharath Sharma and Daniel Burkly

Day 1

For decades now, Jeff Bezos, Amazon founder and CEO, has been reminding internal and external stakeholders that it is always "Day 1" at Amazon.[1]

Day 1 represents the early stage of a company's life when growth and innovation are typically at their peak. Amazon's culture promotes a sense of urgency that you would expect in a start-up, but not necessarily in one of the largest companies in the world.

What does Day 2 look like?

According to Bezos, "Day 2 is stasis. Followed by irrelevance. Followed by excruciating, painful decline. Followed by death. And that is why it is always Day 1."

Amazon began as a 1990s dot-com internet start-up, selling books from Bezos's garage. Since that time, Amazon has evolved into a technology conglomerate with operations in a wide range of industries—retail, grocery, health, and film, to name a few.

Two of Bezos's four essentials for a Day 1 mindset are high-velocity decision making, and embracing external trends.

High-velocity decision making

According to Bezos, "Day 2 companies make high-quality decisions, but they make them *slowly*." The following are some of the ways Bezos recommends enabling rapid decision making.

- *Recognize decisions with two-way doors.* Distinguish between decisions that are reversible (Bezos refers to these as two-way doors) and those that are not. For those that are reversible, a faster, more streamlined decision-making process is appropriate.
- *Don't wait to have 100% of the information.* You can typically make decisions with 70%.
- *Disagree and commit.* If one or more individuals disagree with the rest of their colleagues, the group does not necessarily need to reach consensus; they can disagree but still commit to moving forward, genuinely supporting the decision.
- *Recognize true misalignment issues.* Sometimes teams have different objectives and fundamentally different views; recognize this early and escalate for a resolution.

In some cases, making rapid decisions can lead to failure. Amazon has seen its share of failure over time—the Amazon Fire Phone being a prime example. What mitigates the potential costs of failure is the ability to change direction rapidly. According to Bezos, "If you're good at course correcting, being wrong may be less costly than you think, whereas being slow is going to be expensive for sure."[2]

Embracing external trends

"The outside world can push you into Day 2 if you won't or can't embrace powerful trends quickly. If you fight them, you're probably fighting the future. Embrace them and you have a tailwind," writes Bezos.

Despite becoming a large company, Amazon has consistently embraced external trends—from the early days of e-commerce (when the company was selling books online) to the early days of machine learning and artificial intelligence (when the company developed its AI assistant, Alexa).

Whole Foods

Amazon's acquisition and integration of Whole Foods in 2017 exemplifies the company's embracing external trends and high-velocity decision making. Amazon perceived a need to have both an online presence and physical locations in retail. For example, the company started opening physical bookstores in 2015 after selling online exclusively for almost two decades. Amazon continued this trend of combining online and physical locations in groceries. Further, Amazon sought to capitalize on the growing trend of meal-delivery services, pairing its distribution capabilities with high-end ingredients from Whole Foods.

Amazon and Whole Foods began discussing the US$13.7 billion acquisition only one month before the deal was announced. Having made a quick decision to buy Whole Foods, Amazon began executing on integration plans just as swiftly. Immediately after closing on the acquisition, Amazon decreased prices selectively in Whole Foods stores and put its private-label products onto Amazon's online platform, both of which significantly boosted sales for the combined organization.[3]

In a rapidly transforming world, value for many companies is eroded by slow or incomplete decisions, second-guessing decisions during execution, and implementing good decisions slowly or incompletely. High-velocity decision making and embracing external trends are both critical to creating value by capitalizing on change. What lessons should every company take away? For sustained success, the critical parts of an organization—*strategy, finance, and operations* (SFO)—have to work together seamlessly.

Strategy, finance, and operations integration

SFO represents the key internal stakeholder groups that assess, make, and implement mission-critical decisions within organizations.

We focus on the primary executive activities that make up SFO:

- Developing the company's direction, defining priorities, and establishing initiatives.
- Managing the company's finances and acting as the custodians of capital.
- Making and selling products or services, and getting them to customers efficiently.

SFO components must integrate more and better than they ever have in the past because the pace of change has accelerated dramatically and the complexity of that change has increased significantly. Figure 10.1 depicts the evolution of SFO integration over the past several decades. There was a time when disruption was rare and industry boundaries were stable. The strategy group could formulate a plan and hand it off to finance, who created the budget; then the operations team made and shipped the product. A few companies still operate in this sequential manner today, but they tend to be in businesses that are insulated by patents or regulation.

The seeds of SFO integration began in the 1990s, with globalization, accelerating technological developments and ever-demanding investors. These trends forced more *collaboration* across SFO; for example, strategy needed to make sure manufacturing networks and supply chains could deliver the right products in each country.

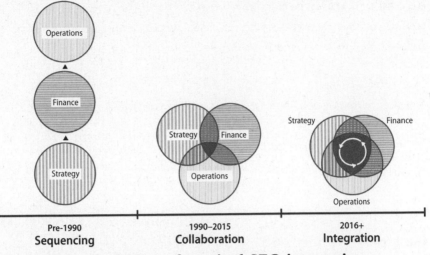

Figure 10.1   Evolution of required SFO integration

The true SFO integration that's required today embodies three characteristics:

1. *Holistic and seamless.* All elements are included and work together as a single team.
2. *In real time.* High-velocity decision making must be a core competency.
3. *In parallel.* Elements do not work sequentially with handoffs or teaming only at the margins.

It is important to note that the three SFO components are not necessarily entirely based in the corporate headquarters; key members are often located in various countries and plants. This geographic distribution of resources enhances their influence within the organization because they are able to penetrate more broadly and deeply.

The key decisions facing a company require the collective input of executives across SFO. Implementing these decisions relies on all three stakeholder groups. In addition, measuring the outcomes and deciding whether tweaks are necessary for the future also falls to SFO. Converting external trends into value quickly requires that an integrated SFO:

- Senses them early enough to act.
- Forms hypotheses on which new business models could be profitable.
- Tests new ideas, fails fast, and learns across the company.
- Doubles down on the winners and begins the process over again.

Complex change will be a constant

The drivers of change are numerous, different from prior years, and evolving rapidly (see Figure 10.2). Though these drivers create stress for an organization, they also offer unprecedented opportunity—provided that SFO is nimble enough to make and execute on decisions quickly.

If these pressures cause each SFO function to focus only on its individual mandate, the resulting dysfunction could well mean lost opportunities and even the demise of the company. Business leaders need to adapt the core of their organizations not just to face off against external pressures but to effectively embrace and use change to build extraordinary shareholder value.

The quality of SFO integration has a direct effect on how successfully your company takes advantage of transformative opportunities, confronts market stresses, and reacts to daily challenges. Some important examples are:

- *Embracing technological disruption.* As we discuss in Chapter 12, to become a truly digital company, the CEO needs to lead. Mastering the seven dimensions such as mapping customer journeys, aligning supply chains, and monetizing data requires tenacious SFO integration.

Primary drivers	New drivers	Examples
• Digitization of demand and supply nodes • Globalization of markets and shifting demographics • Regulatory ebbs and flows by country • Demanding, aggressive investors	• Availability of data and analytical tools to better predict outcomes • New customers, new preferences, less loyalty • Industry convergence undermining conventional performance metrics • Shaping—not just adapting to— change to maximize shareholder value	• Markets created for augmented reality, robotics, and 3-D printing • Consumer demand for organic, natural, locally sourced food and beverages • Ride-sharing companies disrupting the transportation industry • Idle capital eroding enterprise value

Figure 10.2   Drivers of change

- *Celebrating experimentation and learning from failures.* Risk aversion frequently leads to mediocre performance in today's dynamic business environment. As innovation comes more and more from testing new business models, it's important for SFO to be in sync.
- *Acquisitions.* M&A fails for many reasons, often related to insufficient SFO integration. In each phase of the transaction life cycle—from target identification through synergy capture—all functions need to work together in real time. See Chapter 5.
- *Divestments.* Divesting is even more complex than acquiring, so without proper SFO integration, starting with portfolio management, you're unlikely to extract full value. See Chapters 4 and 6.

SFO integration creating value through M&A

Let's look at another real-life example, where M&A figures prominently in capitalizing on external trends. Danaher is a medical, industrial, and commercial products manufacturer with its roots dating back to the early 1980s in its current form. It has developed a diverse portfolio of businesses that serve diagnostics, life sciences, dental, environmental, and applied solutions markets. Danaher ranks in the 95th percentile of all publicly traded US companies in total shareholder return (TSR) over the past 30 years.[4]

To achieve this level of TSR over an extended period of time, Danaher has applied various value levers, including organic growth, geographic expansion, M&A, operational efficiency, and payout policy. It has been one of the most acquisitive companies over the past 30 years, completing more than 400 acquisitions. In our view, the company's M&A process has been a crucial value lever and embodies SFO integration.

As we discussed in Chapter 5, it is difficult to create value with conventional M&A. One recent study of 2,500 mergers and acquisitions showed that more than 60% of those transactions destroyed shareholder value for the acquirer.[5] In our experience, this is often due to the lack of disciplined, repeatable processes enabled by SFO integration. Successful M&A requires all critical functions to work together across the transaction life cycle, in particular to capture synergies. Danaher's M&A approach supports the company's TSR performance.

Danaher's M&A strategy is to identify large global markets with strong growth profiles and low cyclicality, and then acquire companies that will enable a sustainable competitive advantage through brands and technologies. Danaher looks for businesses with branded products that have pricing power, but are not optimally managed. These companies rely heavily on their brands and technologies, but do not focus sufficiently on manufacturing, supply chain, and enterprise functions such as finance and talent management.[6] From the SFO perspective, Danaher applies its integrated model to the companies it acquires, thereby unlocking value in its acquisition targets.

At Danaher, SFO operates in a highly integrated manner, with each group taking collective and individual accountability for various aspects of each transaction.

- Strategy and finance screen potential acquisitions for high profitability and low capital intensity. One of Danaher's key metrics is ROIC; in the past, the company has publicly indicated a minimum hurdle rate of 10% within three years on average.[7]
- Operations and finance assess and measure the financial benefits of potential synergies and operational improvements (to manufacturing; supply chain; selling, general, and administrative [SG&A]; etc.) through implementation of what the company refers to as the Danaher Business System (DBS). DBS represents Danaher's philosophy of continuous improvement throughout the company, including areas such as quality, delivery, cost, and innovation, among others.[8]
- SFO stakeholders build a plan for the first 100 days of ownership, creating alignment with operational improvement priorities and financial objectives.[9] In addition to improving margins for many acquisitions, Danaher has consistently grown revenue through go-to-market investments and new product launches at the acquired businesses.

Concurrent transformational events require a bold vision and significant integration among SFO stakeholders to be successful. On the same day in May 2015, Danaher announced that it was both making one of its largest acquisitions—a US$13.8 billion takeover of Pall Corporation—and spinning off its industrial businesses into a new publicly traded company, later named Fortive Corporation. The decisions to acquire Pall and spin off Fortive have been well received by the market; in the three years following the 13 May 2015 announcement, the cumulative TSR for the combined companies was close to 60%, versus 40% for the S&P 500 Index.[10]

Danaher tracks and communicates to the market both the degree and pace of its portfolio transformation. In the company's "Investor & Analyst Day" presentation at the end of 2017, management noted that operating companies acquired since 2011 represented more than 50% of Danaher's revenue—an example of achieving the results you explicitly target.

How urgent is your need for SFO integration?

Use these four indicators to help gauge your industry's pace of change, and therefore how critically you need to drive SFO integration:

- Churn among the top three players over the past two years.
- Differential effects of data, digitalization, and analytics on individual competitors.
- Rapid evolution in customer preferences.
- Widening of the shareholder value gap between the industry leader and the next tier of competitors.

Stress testing your SFO integration

We suggest a self-assessment across six categories to evaluate the extent of SFO integration at your company:

1. Governance and decision making

- Are SFO functions viewed as equals within the organization?
- Does it typically take less than three months to make substantial investment decisions?

- Are decisions typically made without delays caused by requests for further analysis?
- Do you escalate decisions when there is a fundamental lack of alignment rather than trying to reach consensus?
- Do you differentiate between decisions that are reversible (and therefore carry less risk) versus those that are not?
- Is accountability shared among functions and are respective goals clear, particularly beyond the C-suite?

2. Strategic planning

- Does the strategic planning process include long-term (e.g. five-year) and medium-term (e.g. two-year) horizons?
- Do you monitor the pace of business portfolio change?
- Do your effectiveness measures include assessing the company's performance versus that of the industry leader, for example, in both market share and wallet share?
- Are senior executives from each of the SFO functions core participants in the process?

3. Capital planning

- Is there a formal committee that oversees capital planning and capital allocation?
- Are senior executives from each SFO function on the committee?
- Do your periodic portfolio reviews involve senior SFO members?

4. Innovation, including R&D

- Is there an innovation or R&D council with a charter to increase revenue from new products and services?
- Do the measures of your council's effectiveness include:

- ○ Concept–to–product market launch time?
- ○ Pace of new product introduction?
- ○ Success of new products?
- ○ Entry into new categories?
- ○ Rationalization (e.g. discontinuance) of products?
- ■ Are senior executives from each of the SFO functions on the council?

5. Sales and operations planning

- ■ Is there a sales and operations planning (S&OP) council that includes demand strategy and supply chain strategy in its charter, in addition to tactical sales and production planning?
- ■ Do measures of the council's effectiveness include increasing market share and increasing gross margin?
- ■ Does the council include the heads of strategy, finance-commercial, finance-supply chain, and supply chain?

6. Transactions

- ■ Is SFO involved, with appropriate roles, from the start of each transaction (acquisitions, joint ventures, and divestments)?
- ■ Is accountability clear among SFO constituents for each phase of the transaction, for example, deal origination, due diligence, structuring, deal close, and integration?
- ■ Do you usually win desirable acquisition targets from fast-moving competitors?

If you answered "No" to more than a few of these questions, there are likely areas where your company would benefit from increased SFO integration.

It's a journey, not a destination

There are elements of the Capital Agenda that have well-defined end points—acquisitions and divestments, for example. In contrast, SFO integration is not something you can or should finish; it is an area for continuous improvement. The pursuit is well worth the effort: SFO integration has the potential to make your organization one that not only adapts and benefits from change, but actually shapes the change with which competitors must find ways to cope.

Notes

1. Amazon 2016 Annual Letter to Shareholders.
2. Ibid.
3. Rich Duprey, "Early Evidence That the Amazon-Whole Foods Merger Is a Picture Perfect Marriage," *The Motley Fool*, 26 September 2017, https://www.fool.com/investing/2017/09/26/early-evidence-that-the-amazon-whole-foods-merger.aspx.
4. EY analysis of Capital IQ data.
5. L.E.K. Consulting LLC, "Mergers & Acquisitions: What Winners Do to Beat the Odds," 2013.
6. PwC, "Danaher's Instruments of Change," *Strategy+Business* 82 (Spring 2016).
7. Danaher Corporation 2001 Annual Report.
8. "Danaher 2017 Investor & Analyst Day," 14 December 2017, http://investors.danaher.com/events-presentations.
9. PwC, "Danaher's Instruments of Change," *Strategy+Business* 82 (Spring 2016).
10. EY analysis of Capital IQ data.

11

How can you get the most out of your advisors?

Giri Varadarajan and Aayush Tulsyan

Successful automotive equipment companies must focus on three goals: winning new customers, retaining existing customers, and maintaining customer satisfaction through the life cycle of equipment ownership.

A global industry player was struggling to achieve these goals in Japan, and called in our colleagues from the United States to analyze its 160+ dealers in Japan and to work with them to develop an effective solution. The expected thing to do in this situation would be to hire a local advisor that understands the language, culture, and business.

Why hire advisors from the United States to help fix a problem in Japan? The client concluded that it had the required local business and cultural knowledge; however, it lacked sufficient process expertise and the ability to design and implement a standardized solution across the country—so it sourced the optimum talent globally. The client arrived at this decision after thoroughly evaluating its strengths and weaknesses, and clearly defining what it wanted from an advisor (more about this later in the chapter). EY worked with the client to develop a balanced scorecard at the outset of the project to define what success would look like for the dealer business. This helped keep everyone focused on the same goals, even with cultural and language differences.

The effort began by building trust rather than launching a national project. We developed a hypothesis, conducted interviews, and framed initial recommendations based on these learnings and our past experiences. This process gave the client an opportunity to assess us as an advisor and possibly even as a journey partner[1]—a distinction we'll cover later.

As the project progressed from design to implementation support, we shifted our team mix to a larger proportion of local members, who would be more adept at change management and working with local and regional dealers to roll out these changes. This helped the client achieve a successful implementation of the project across Japan.

Setting the context

Let's address the elephant in the room: we're advisors, and this is a chapter about how to work with advisors. You might expect we would be unqualified advocates for hiring advisors, but our recommendations are more nuanced.

It would be bad and less credible advice if we said, "You definitely need advisors." The proper answer is that it depends on the problem you need to solve or the opportunity you want to capture.

We will explore good and bad reasons, as well as mistakes, such as hiring advisors prematurely and keeping them too long. This chapter will give you advice about getting advice, and put it in the context of optimizing your Capital Agenda.

First principles

It's important not to confuse "getting advice" with "getting advisors." We all get advice daily—whether solicited or not. The problem is that sometimes you need to go beyond casual suggestions and make substantial progress toward a defined goal. That's when you might consider getting an advisor.

A Fortune 100 senior executive whom we greatly respect, and who has worked with many consultants, has this to say about why to hire an advisor:

> At the end of the day, the only reason to hire an advisor is to change the outcome of a situation, whether it's an opportunity or a crisis. You do that by getting an advisor whose proven methodology is directly applicable to the problem you'd like to solve.

Other executives who've successfully used advisors do so:

- To get an unbiased, outside-in assessment of a situation.
- To confirm—or question—the feasibility of a proposed solution.
- To receive insights and perspectives based on expertise and experience.
- To help apply leading practices in order to solve a problem.
- To help an organization raise its capabilities to a higher level.

You should not expect to get a so-called answer or silver bullet from a good advisor. If that's what you're looking for, you may be making a mistake. What you get from an advisor are insights, coupled with strategic thinking, that challenge the status quo. What's more important is that you get a set of capabilities to help navigate your organization through a complex situation. With the help of the advisor, you co-create the thing you're trying to get done, and that goes well beyond an "answer."

A highly underappreciated element of working with an advisor is the methodology that an advisor brings to the project. You should not be buying merely advice. The right methodology can help to unlock the creativity and insight of your internal team. It also helps to structure and organize the work, which helps turn insight into actionable strategy. That then supports the outcomes you're looking for. More on this later.

When it is appropriate—and not appropriate—to use an advisor

When do you know that it's time to bring in an advisor?

You can do just about anything yourself without advisors. But getting an advisory firm on board can help in certain specific ways. Then again, some situations may seem like the time to bring in an advisor, but are not. Let's look at various scenarios (refer to Figure 11.1).

Every situation falls into one of four quadrants:

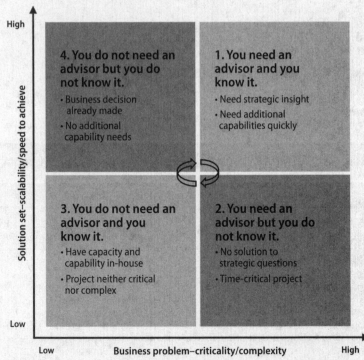

Figure 11.1 When is it appropriate—and not appropriate—to use an advisor?

1. You need an advisor and you know it

To get strategic insight. You are at the crossroads of choosing a strategic option or making another important decision. You conclude that it would be helpful to have someone guide—and occasionally force—you to thoroughly think through the alternatives, using a proven approach. An advisor can clarify and help establish benchmark criteria for success, and assess your ability to acquire and maintain those capabilities.

To accelerate a process. You're in a relatively new market and have captured modest market share, but now that market is heating up, with new, cash-rich competitors. How can you reconfigure your supply chain and commercial model to gain much greater market share in the next 12 months?

You need additional capabilities quickly. You have a line of successful consumer packaged goods in Europe, and want to explore expanding that line into Latin America. You learned the European market on your own and could do the same with Latin America—given enough time—but the window of opportunity doesn't allow that luxury.

2. You need an advisor but you do not know it

You've wrestled for a long time with certain strategic questions without coming to a resolution. They may involve concerns around restructuring, disruptions in your industry, a steady erosion of margin, or other value-depleting trends.

You have no data about how long certain initiatives should take and what they should involve (such as entering a new market), and you're not sure how to go about finding the right solution.

You're in a downward spiral of cost cutting and are unable to invest in technologies, people, or advisors who might get you out of the slump. This situation leads to more cost cutting.

You're struggling with breaking down the situation and defining the specific questions to be answered.

You need a specific set of analytics capabilities and tool set during the due diligence period, and you don't have this internally.

3. You do not need an advisor and you know it

- A project has ended.
- You've built robust capacity and capability in-house.
- You're able to staff up and down without creating problems.
- The project is neither critical nor complex.
- You have sufficient time to execute your plans.

4. You do not need an advisor but you do not know it

An executive might say: "I've decided to buy Acme Industries. I'm making my offer next week and I need a second opinion because I think I may get a lot of pushback from my board." If the decision has already been made, then the advisor's ability to add value will be limited. However, if the advisor is given the freedom and information to provide an independent and objective perspective, then such a second opinion may be useful.

You should be hiring advisors because they do things differently from the way you do them. They should not be brought in to rubber-stamp decisions already made, or to manage corporate politics. Confirmatory advice can be helpful (or even necessary) from a governance perspective, but you should be wary of paying someone to tell you things you already know. Advisors would have been more valuable if they had been brought in upstream from the decision to buy Acme, at the stage when they could help explore options. Early on is the time to ask focusing questions:

- Given your strategic objectives, where is your next big opportunity?
- Are there organic growth options to achieve your goals?

- What are the industry trends you're seeing, and which opportunities are you uniquely positioned to harvest?
- What company could you potentially buy, or partner with? How does Acme fit into that picture?

It's also okay to hire an advisor if Acme is in play and you want to think through quickly whether it makes sense to do a deal there, but not because you've already decided and want a second opinion. Maybe you're already down the road in the decision to purchase Acme, and want someone to help you with contractual protections, valuation, negotiations, integration, tax structuring, and so on. That could be an appropriate time to hire an advisor for expertise in those areas.

Let's say you're understaffed in a country and you think that maybe the advisor can be your arms and legs on that project. Advisors should be hired to apply their proven processes to your business objectives, and not as additional full-time equivalents (FTEs) on your staff, unless it's for a true short-term engagement to keep time lines moving.

Staff augmentation is a perfectly legitimate activity. A large advisory firm might even have units that perform that role, and they may do it well. What's important is to recognize when you're hiring an advisor for the ability to support decision making, and when you're hiring someone in order to augment staff.

Hiring process

It's not uncommon for companies to select an advisory firm through a process that somewhat resembles the TV talent show model. Companies send out a request for proposal (RFP) to multiple firms, ask for written responses, and then schedule presentations by those firms. Sometimes several advisors will be given 90-minute windows to present, and are stacked back-to-back during one long day. At the end of that marathon, the client chooses an advisor.

That serves the best interests of neither the client nor the advisors. Most such talent shows provide only a superficial understanding of client objectives and the advisors' capabilities.

Some small amount of this process may be unavoidable, in the sense that multiple firms are reviewed in a short period. However, if you're moving into an unfamiliar space, the best way to decide on an advisor is to meet people from the relevant firms in a less-than-formal setting. Explain your business objectives, and then tell the advisors a little bit about what you're doing and why.

Then have them provide some initial thoughts and insights. As the client, you should be listening for three things:

1. Would I enjoy working with this person?
2. Can I see myself being vulnerable in front of this person? That may sound like an odd question, but in reality if you're going to benefit from advice, you need to be humble enough to receive it. Is this person somebody that I could have a good enough rapport with that I could handle getting frank advice from him or her? Can I be comfortable enough with this person to have productive back-and-forth interaction to effectively handle necessary course corrections?
3. Would the advice be worth taking? In other words, what is the quality of the advice, based not only on the person's experience, but also on the experience and capabilities of the team around him or her? Does this person have the substance to help me move into some area that's new to me?

What I'd next like to hear from the advisor during our conversations is something along the lines of "Okay, I answered the questions that your procurement process required. I addressed the scope of the project as it has been outlined. What I'd like to do now is have a chance to recommend some things that I would either limit or suggest you modify in the scoping document, in order for this to turn into a successful business outcome." These additional elements might be insights or perspectives gained from the advisor's experience, and this sort of response indicates independent thinking and ownership of the project. Can the advisor also start to anticipate some of the critical implications that may be outside this engagement but will be a result of the course of action?

This would also tell me I'm not just being told what someone thinks I want to hear. The advisor may indeed have a vision, strategic thinking, and methodology that's different from my preconceived notions, and that may produce better results for us. Remember, you're hiring advisors because they bring expertise and perspectives you don't have in-house.

Don't choose advisors based on the lowest cost, but instead on the best value in terms of the right fit, capability, and experience they bring to the engagement. In the long run, this approach will help you to avoid cost overruns, dead ends, and lost value. Getting the right advice, in a timely manner, will almost always be more cost effective than having an unsuccessful or inefficient project drag on at a low hourly rate.

Speaking of the engagement, you need to have as clear a statement as possible about its scope and nature, including what success looks like in terms of your key desired outcomes. Advisors run the gamut from strategy firms to ones that encompass major areas like operations and finance, and to ones with highly specialized expertise in crisis management, cybersecurity, and so on. The proper match between you and an advisor can be made only when your problem statement and desired outcome are as clear as you can make them.

How to do proper due diligence on advisors

Your personal network is larger than you think it is. That's true for everyone. Social media business tools are surprisingly powerful not only for contacting your connections, but also for doing quick research about who knows whom. Often just one or two well-placed emails can get you in touch with people who have a wealth of information on the advisors you're considering.

Ask the advisor to give you an overview of how he or she would approach your challenges, including a description of their methodology. That might also include a 90-minute workshop for a handful of people on your team. During the workshop, the advisor should walk you through an example of a similar project that the company did, including what went well and what could have been done better.

The advisor should be able to provide sufficiently anonymized case studies that convey the team's approach and expertise without disclosing the name or identifiable details of the actual client being discussed. In many cases adequate anonymization can be achieved by changing names, statistics, locations, and organizational structure, while preserving enough of the methodology and insight to demonstrate real-life expertise. Experienced advisors tend to publish white papers, case studies, special reports, articles, and books. Take the opportunity to look at what's published, and study the tone. Are you reading material that contains generic information or real insights? Does the material simply describe what the advisor did on projects, or does it cover specific business outcomes?

Ask to speak with other clients who have worked with the advisor. Your questions can cover some of the areas we've just listed; for example: What is the advisor's methodology? To what degree did the advisor make you think hard about topics, and maybe even challenge you? What are the advisor's strengths and not-so-strong areas?

Then ask to speak with some of the team members who will be doing the day-to-day work on the project. It's important to understand their capabilities and gauge their ability to deliver unbiased advice, rather than merely accept whatever you say.

Advisors as competitors and as peers

This is a good place to bring up the topic of other advisors, first in the context of competition.

As part of your due diligence and interviewing process, ask: "Whom do you see as your competition?" That simple question sometimes can speak volumes.

What you don't want to hear is "Oh, it's my policy not to say anything negative about the competition, but instead to stick to the topic of how I can help you." To which you should respond, "I don't want you to say anything that's untruthful about your competitors, but I do want to hear how you differ from them in specific ways."

Then ask: "What do you do really well that you're particularly proud of? What are some areas where your competition does things either differently or perhaps even better? If you were working on this project and a couple of areas were outside your sweet spot, how would you suggest we go about getting someone else to help with that, and what's your recommended path for working with them?"

These last questions will tell you a lot about the advisor. Is this person unwilling to admit that anyone comes even close in ability, or has strengths in other areas? Does the advisor look surprised at the question and then say that the only circumstance where there could be another advisor brought in is if this advisor controls the other as a subcontractor? In our experience, these sorts of defensive responses tend to foreshadow problems down the road.

On the other hand, you may find that the advisor is both experienced and humble. "We're strong in cross-border taxation, but not as strong in the evolving area of cryptocurrencies. If you need both, then you may want to bring in someone that specializes in crypto work. We can walk you through where we have effectively teamed up with other advisors to bring the best business outcomes to the situation."

If you as the client have clearly stated the business outcomes you need, then having more than one advisor—with equally clearly stated areas of responsibility—means that the advisors should not trip over each other.

Note: Don't be the client who says (and we're not making this up): "I want a single throat to choke across bankers, attorneys, and advisors." Sometimes complicated business outcomes require the insight and support of multiple organizations. An experienced, high-quality advisor almost certainly will not agree to be that single throat, because the statement may be indicative of a predisposition to assign blame instead of working through difficult issues. Of course, it's perfectly acceptable—and a leading practice—to insist that an advisor provide a single point of coordination across his or her own work streams. While good advisors will normally resist taking responsibility for another advisor's work, they can provide project management support to help you keep the process on track.

How to start the relationship with an advisor

Let's say you've navigated the process and have chosen an advisor. What's the best way to begin to work together for the first time? Is it to dive right into your big project, or to create some type of pilot project to see how things work?

We suggest neither approach. Instead, we recommend that the main project for which you hired the advisor be broken into natural stages. Let's take an integration, for example. You've decided to buy a company and need to do some planning around finance and operations before you make the final offer. That would be one natural stage of the project.

The next stage might be the period from "sign to close," followed by "close to Day 100" and so on. Then you could say to the advisor, "I would like to know your total capabilities and your general approach to the project. But I'd like to see the work broken into discrete phases. As we transition from one phase to the next, I want to do two things: reflect on how well we're working together, and also build some capabilities internally."

Each stage is unique and separate, but part of the overall project. Obviously you have the right to change horses at the next stage, but that's not the reason you're working in stages. The objective instead is to be able to have outcomes to evaluate and learn from at each stage.

Fourteen other leading practices (and what not to do) when hiring and managing advisors

1. *Be very careful about allowing middle managers complete freedom when hiring advisors.* You may think: "I want my middle management to take ownership." If they have never experienced this type of project or transformation, then it's a recipe for problems. Advisors could also be perceived as a threat because they might make middle management look bad. Sometimes not the best people get hired, and even if they are the best, they may be constrained in ways that do not maximize their value. At the very least, plan to stay involved in this crucial process to ensure that advisors are given enough freedom to provide the right advice, and that their input is carefully considered.

2. *Do not set arbitrary constraints.* Criteria like "We want to use the advisors that are local to a given region" are not productive. The problem is that advisors are not interchangeable commodities; you want the right team for the specific job. Region-specific expertise may be an important consideration, but not the only one.

3. *Do not consider the advisory staff as a static entity.* Few aspects of business are static. In most projects, the advisory team size and composition will evolve as phases change. For example, an acquisition advisory team may have a relatively large number of tax structuring specialists early on. In the later phase of the project there may be fewer of those experts and more people focused on operational integration.

4. *Be sure to align incentives.* You're asking for problems if your people are incentivized in one direction (lowering unit costs in your plants, for example) but your advisor might come back with recommendations that are counter to those incentives—such as lowering inventory levels to free up cash. The CFO is usually best positioned to balance these forces, and can be an active coach to middle managers, who work and drive the project on a daily basis.

5. *After you've hired an advisor, listen to her or him.* Provide the advisor with as much access to people and information as you can. Treat the advisor with the same courtesy as you do your own employees. You co-own with that advisor the performance and business outcomes.

6. *Watch for scope creep.* Continue to be as clear as you can about what you want to accomplish, and be on the lookout for the sorts of conversations that cause scope creep. If you start to think that may be happening, step back and make sure that you understand the time and money implications of the contemplated changes. They can be okay as long as you have regular, robust discussions at both strategic and operational levels. Everyone from executive sponsor to middle managers needs to be part of this dialogue, and the scope should be modified only with great care.

7. *Continue to learn about the advisor's methodology,* and work on complementing each other's skills. Don't tell the advisor how to run his or her process and what set of tools to bring to solve the problem. If it turns out you don't like the process, it's time to hire a different advisor.

8. *Review the knowledge transfer every three to six months,* depending on the project phase and level of activity. Make sure you're letting advisors know that you will ask, "How are you transferring best practices and knowledge to us, so they become part of our routine?" Good advisors want to do that because they are looking to build long-term relationships.

9. *Regularly evaluate whether you are able to take over this project internally.* Have you met your original objectives? By the way, if you have, then be sure to highlight any standout performance on the part of the advisor. Praise is rare and valued, even when it's completely deserved.

10. *Know when it's time to end the project.* A good advisor will come to you and say, "You don't need us for this work anymore." It's

a matter of protecting the advisor's brand. That's better than making you feel later that you were strung along and now don't want to hire that advisor again. From the advisor's viewpoint, a strong long-term relationship is more valuable than an incremental one-time fee.

11. *Be alert to the nature of surprises.* Has the advisor surprised you? Examples of a good "yes" are beating deadlines and delivering exceptional quality in terms of thoroughness and ease of use. Examples of a bad "yes" are unexpected fees or expenses, not delivering what was expected, and not proactively communicating when circumstances changed. Assessing the nature of surprises is one good way to know if it's time to end the engagement—or to consider moving forward and deepening the relationship.

12. *Codify learnings.* It is a good sign if your advisor takes the initiative to create a document with lessons learned, or a playbook to help you with similar projects in the future.

13. *Periodically review scope, team size, and budget.* Does the advisor manage your money as if it's theirs? Good advisors should sometimes be able to return unused budget dollars if they've managed the project well.

14. *Have open discussions beyond the current engagement.* What has the advisor observed and learned about the business and organization? What opportunities or threats does the advisor see that may not be on your radar?

Beyond advisors to journey partners

At the beginning of this chapter, we talked about the difference between advice and advisors. Now we'd like to make some further important distinctions.

You say to a vendor: "I need a knee brace."

You say to an advisor: "I have a knee issue."

You say to a *journey partner:* "I didn't even know I had a condition; thanks for the early diagnosis."

In the business world, all three functions are important and necessary. If you need a fairness opinion for an upcoming transaction, you go to someone who in that instance plays the role of a vendor. You get the opinion and are done.

With an advisor you want to develop a deeper, ongoing, and mutually beneficial relationship. You know each other's strengths and weaknesses. You have a communication level where the advisor feels okay saying: "What were you thinking there?!" or "I think you might be looking at this backward; here's a whole different explanation for what you just described."

If you and an advisor do in fact mesh and work at the relationship, it can grow from the one-off engagement to a series of projects. You should be able to tell during that first project if the trajectory is headed in the right direction.

With some time and a bit of luck, the ongoing advisory relationship may turn into that of a journey partner. This builds on the advisor role, but with a deeper level of trust on both sides. It's a go-to person for some of your toughest questions and challenges.

You can pick up the phone and call your journey partner, and ask: "Hey, Mary, I'm confronting a new situation, and I'd like to get your perspective and help on it." Mary is not starting the consulting clock, because your relationship is deeper than something that's measured in billable minutes. Instead, she might come back with, "Okay, but what do you mean by 'help'? Is this help with a decision, or help with thinking through options?"

You might describe a situation where a group of managers are feeling threatened, and you need some creative solution in order to both translate strategy to action and create a win for middle management. The two of you might explore a number of options, and reach a few dead ends as well as viable scenarios. Your journey partner may even say, "I get where you're going and what you need.

We're qualified for about 50% of this project, but you should talk to another firm about the areas we don't specialize in; let me introduce you to them."

A journey partner relationship is rare but absolutely worth pursuing because of the high-value insights and perspectives it can bring to your most difficult challenges.

Notes

1. The term *journey partner* refers to an informal relationship, not a formal legal one.

12 | Can your strategy thrive in a digital world?

Tony Qui and Glenn Engler

It started with a straightforward question. Someone in the Starbucks marketing department in 2010 asked: "Wouldn't it be great if we had one of those prepaid, stored-value cards?"

Starbucks created one. That soon led to another enhancement, which was a loyalty program: after customers bought several drinks, they could get a free latte or other drink. Then the program grew into one with the ability to send gift cards, because one in seven adults receives gift cards during the holidays.

Soon thereafter the card became a mobile phone app, and the focus turned to improving the customer experience in Starbucks stores. Starbucks found that when mobile pay solutions were offered, three things happened: it was more convenient and faster for many customers to pay that way; order details were conveyed more effectively because the customer entered the specifics of the order; and it increased the throughput or number of customers a store could serve at peak periods by more than 10%, mainly because the customer didn't have to search for exact change to hand the barista.

Speaking of baristas, Starbucks studied what was the biggest determinant of whether a customer would return to a store, and it was the barista. Does the person know you? Is he or she smiling? If so, most customers would come back. If the place is going crazy with orders and lines are moving slowly, customers usually don't come back as quickly. Therefore, Starbucks went from improving the customer experience to looking at how baristas could be freed up from certain tasks so they could spend that time interacting with customers and improving the customer experience.

It's like a digital horizon. You move forward and solve one problem, and now you see other opportunities on the horizon that you couldn't see before, according to the company. Starbucks is now spending roughly 40% of its efforts on digital activities. Critical intellectual property used to be things like a recipe for a beverage. Now it's become an algorithm that predicts customers' propensity to buy, based on hundreds of customer preferences tracked by Starbucks.

Among the next challenges Starbucks is tackling: how to leverage real-time data to suggest alternative locations for faster service, based on up-to-the-moment assessment of lines and throughput times.

Extending the reach of digital

We're so far past why "digital" is the trend for the future, you need no convincing.

We suspect you may be thinking: "My company is already digital. We have been all along. In fact, we were an early adopter. What can you possibly tell me that I don't already know?"

This chapter won't try to convince you that digital technologies are important and worth investing in; you know that already. It's about helping you see that digital is likely much more far-reaching than your organization currently thinks, regardless of your industry. In fact, asking "What is our digital strategy?" these days is too narrow. Rather, companies and their leadership should be asking "What is our business strategy in a digital world?" If you are not, there's a very good chance you're thinking about digital incorrectly.

How can we be so bold?

We suggest you take the next two minutes to consider the following questions. You'll get the very most out of this exercise if you don't look ahead for our take on the answers.

> **Question 1**: Who owns digital at your company? They go by different names, like chief information officer (CIO), chief technology officer (CTO), chief marketing officer (CMO), or maybe even chief digital officer (CDO). The core concern of this question is to help determine who within your company owns digital.
>
> **Answer 1**: If your answer was anything other than CEO, give yourself a zero. To survive the digital transformation, digital cannot be delegated. Although digital needs to be embedded across the organization, because it reaches into every business unit and function, it has to be a critical part of the CEO's mandate.
>
> **Question 2**: What does *digital* mean at your company? Jot down what comes to mind.
>
> **Answer 2**: The typical responses we get are "It's mobile." "It's video." "It's a website." Or "It's the digitization of content."

We say yes it is, for starters. But to thrive, the marketplace now requires you to think about digital across the following seven dimensions (which we'll discuss in more detail later):

1. Customer journeys
2. Supply chain
3. Marketing and sales
4. Automation
5. Data
6. Risk
7. Organic and inorganic investment

You may say, "That describes the entire company." We again would say that you're right.

Look at Figure 12.1.

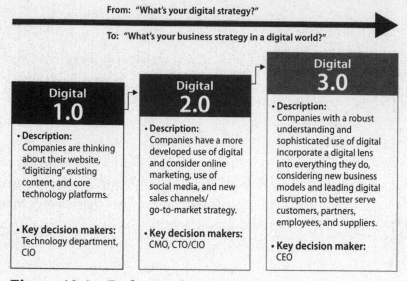

Figure 12.1 Reframe the question

All companies are somewhere in the continuum from Digital 1.0 to 3.0. Also, a single company may not neatly fit into one of the levels, but each business unit may be in a different phase.

To better understand which phase your company is in, consider the following:

Phase 1.0 mindset is *digital = technology*:

"We know we need to capture our data, have a website, and connect our digital systems around the globe."

Phase 2.0 mindset is using digital in marketing, sales, and customer support:

"We have a digital owner who reports to the CMO or CTO. We are aggressively using video, social media, digital marketing, commerce, and predictive analytics to enable our salesforce, build our brands, and drive demand generation and ultimately sales." The company still fundamentally operates the way it always has, but now with a set of digital initiatives.

Phase 3.0 mindset is being defined by digital:

Digital permeates the organization well past the "initiative" stage. It is top-down from the CEO as a core part of her or his strategic mandates, and it is bottom–up throughout every part of the company.

At the phase 2.0 stage, the operative word is *what*, as in: "What do we have? We have a chief digital officer and a new mobile app, and we recently launched new connected devices."

When you're defined by digital in the phase 3.0 mindset, you go beyond the *what* and get to the *who*, the *how*, and the *why*. Who is responsible for digital? Our CEO. How do we make decisions? By regularly stress testing our decisions and direction with specific questions. Why are we so obsessed with this? Because digital is driving dramatic disruption in business models, and fueling new opportunities for traditional and nontraditional competitors alike. More about those later.

Who's the digital disruptor?

Jeff Bezos, founder of Amazon, has this to say:

> *When people say that an entrant is disruptive in an industry, what they really mean is that customers are adopting that new way. At Amazon, we've had a lot of inventions that we were very excited about, and customers didn't care at all. And believe me, those inventions were not disruptive in any way. The only thing that's disruptive is customer adoption. If you can invent a better way, and if customers agree that it's a better way, then they will use that.*[1]

It's therefore useful to look at the fundamental changes in the marketplace from the customer's perspective. The sections below illustrate what we suspect many people think to themselves:

Location

"I don't need to go out and shop; I can shop from my phone or desktop. They'll deliver it wherever I want."

Time

"I used to expect goods to be delivered in weeks or several days, and it was always a range. I now think anything longer than two-day shipping is too long. And more and more I'm hearing about same-day or even two-hour delivery."

"There used to be a handful of airlines, and you needed a travel agent to get the inside scoop on good flights. Now I expect real-time prices, price-drop alerts, and tools that tell me that if I can travel a day earlier or later I can save a bundle. If I want, I can plan every bit of the trip separately based on genuine reviews of airlines, hotels, restaurants, and even Lyft drivers."

Selection

"I'm not limited to what the local store has in terms of colors, sizes, and models. I can get any of them, as long as they're available somewhere, or can be made to order."

"I've moved from essentially being on a local island to being in an international network. Retailers overseas are vying for my business, with very similar delivery times to what the retailers in my city can provide."

"I used to rely on advice from ivory-tower, local 'experts.' My neighborhood doctor told me I had arthritis without even examining me. Now I can rely on huge online resources like the Mayo Clinic and WebMD for professional guidance, not to mention people on YouTube and elsewhere. It turns out I don't have arthritis at all. I'll still go to doctors, but I'm much more informed now."

Two-way reviews

"Of course companies think their products are great, but I rely on crowd-sourced, real-time reviews of products and service providers. You can just tell when it's a fake review or a real one. Besides, Amazon, TripAdvisor, and others allow you to review the reviewers!"

"I pick up a few extra bucks driving for Lyft. I do get reviewed by customers, but I can review them too if they leave my car a mess. It's the same with Airbnb."

Size

"Size mattered in the past. Sears was once everywhere and had the best selection of tools. Now I can go online to Amazon—I don't care where their physical locations are—and sort by reviews. The top result for a highly specialized tool might be a woman making them in her garage workshop."

"I used to play catch-up with getting more storage capacity and computing power for my desktop computer. I played the game of 'What speed is your CPU?' Now no one cares, because the computing is being done in the cloud. Plus companies now hand out terabytes of online storage for free."

"I could tell you in the past who was big. It was the big store down the street, or the big scientific instrument company with the phonebook-sized catalog that got printed once a year. Now I can't tell who's big, because a small company can have a better and more detailed website than a big company. And products from the big and small guys get delivered to me just as quickly. In fact, the small company uses Fulfillment by Amazon and I have its product at just about the time that the big guy is telling me my order 'is in process and will be leaving the warehouse shortly.'"

What has not changed?

- People still have 24 hours in the day.
- They look for shortcuts to get things done.
- They like when they find a product or service on which they can rely.

People still love to be pampered and waited on. Just because a service can be do it yourself (DIY), that doesn't mean the done for you (DFY) market has gone away. Look at the explosion of home delivery for meal kits, wardrobe outfit packs, and the like. Make it easy and tell a great story, and many people will pay extra for that.

Focus on seven dimensions of digital

It's pretty clear that customer expectations are disrupting traditional business. So how can you grab more than your fair share of the market by having the phase 3.0 mindset that's defined by digital? We suggest that you focus on the following seven areas:

1. Outline your customer journeys

Most companies have a handle on their core customer segments. What we have discovered is that most of their perspectives are static, rearview-mirror-based instead of forward-looking.

Push the boundaries from the current state to the ideal end state. How do customers do their research for your product or service? Who are the key influencers along the way? What sources and tools do they use? When working with a major entertainment park, we found that while many of their experiences were immersive digital ones, the shopping, researching, ticketing, and fulfillment operations were painfully paper-based. A journey mapping should define seamless experiences, recommendation engines, and embedded commerce tools. These not only should increase speed and ease of use, but allow for moments of "surprise and delight" along the way.

We list customer journeys as the first dimension because they need to guide discussions from the CEO down, on a regular basis. Leadership must address:

- What is frustrating our customers?
- How can we adopt technology from competitors or even from other industries to remove the frustration?
- What can we do to save customers time, money, and stress to the point that they will tell everybody about it?

2. Identify opportunities and threats in your supply chain

Review the websites and offerings of your suppliers in order to determine if they are going directly to your end customers, thus devaluing your leverage.

Keep up with regular advances in logistics, the Internet of Things (IoT) (connected devices), 3D printing (additive manufacturing), artificial intelligence, and other technologies that can reduce down-time, lower operating costs, and shorten delivery times. You don't need to be expert at them, but you do need to be exposed to developments. This will allow your brain to synthesize it all and prompt you to think, "Hey, wait—what if we could use X to do Y in our business?"

3. Monitor marketing and sales channels for changes in how your customers make decisions

It used to be easier: you had a sales force and an advertising/marketing budget, and you drove traffic to your store/website/distribution channel. Now that mechanism is different because so many other factors influence customers.

If you're a sensor manufacturer selling to engineers and designers and have a website with product PDFs and a sales force, what do you do with millennial decision makers who won't come to your website, and instead use expert communities to drive decision making?

Tool-and-die companies have been around for centuries. One such company studied the customer journey and discovered that 71% of its new prospects had done all of their research before they ever talked to salespeople. As a result, this company digitalized its engagement model, not only creating more content than ever before, but distributing it to those places where their prospects researched potential products, instead of waiting to react to a sales call.

Why are video bloggers and influencers so important in many categories like fashion, cosmetics, travel, technology, and financial services? They have large followings who trust their recommendations (over those from manufacturers) because they are often authentic and transparent.

You should research where the conversations and reviews are happening with your customers, and make plans to engage with them there. It's remarkable how many products have terrible (and sometimes highly biased or bogus) reviews on Amazon, yet the seller never engages with reviewers. It's a great opportunity to correct mis-understandings, explain features, and, if necessary, show how you support issues that arise with buyers. These conversations are happening not just at Amazon, but also on product and user forums, social media, and sites like Quora, where people can ask questions of experts. If you sell Business to Business (B2B), don't assume you're protected from social media conversations; take a look at your brand voice and the topics associated with your company on social media. There's a good chance you'll be surprised at how individuals are talking about you.

4. What can you automate?

Of course a major goal of companies in this competitive environment is to maintain margin and drive profitable growth. How are you regularly getting acquainted with automation advances in your industry and in industries from which you can borrow concepts?

Key standard back-office processes such as finance, human resources, sales and marketing, and customer operations are major targets for automation that not only can preserve or improve your margins, but also can align with the DIY desire of many consumers. Aggressively explore robotic process automation (RPA), chatbots, and other technologies that can dramatically change the game.

5. Are you putting data to maximum use?

How has your organization embraced different types of data and analytics?

- Descriptive (historically based analysis)
- Predictive (future outcome and business modeling)
- Prescriptive (operationalization of predictive scenarios)

Are you embedding other technologies like machine learning? How can you further monetize data? What services can be developed to enhance value, margin, and competitive advantage? It may be tempting to think, "We're doing the best we can because we're over-loaded with data," but the goal has to be moving beyond collecting even more data, to driving more insight.

What internal management reports do you regularly review that did not exist two years ago? If you're reviewing basically the same information, you may be standing still in a fast-moving environment.

6. Have you updated your risk assessment in these four areas?

Our approach to risk management goes beyond traditional categories to include cybersecurity, tax, legal, and regulatory, as well as talent and reputation. The need for this holistic view was highlighted when it became apparent that there were political repercussions to sharing one's personal life online, sending social media companies scrambling to adapt their privacy rules—and quite possibly their core business models.

Cybersecurity

Most organizations look at digital risk solely from a cybersecurity lens, because that's what's in the news every day. That is critical, given the abundance of data and the multitude of devices getting con-nected. And as connected devices permeate businesses, organizations have to think about cyber risk not just within their four walls, but in a distributed environment. In other words, your machines are at risk, sitting at your customer sites, embedded with sensors to drive remote diagnostics; they, too, can be the target of hacking.

Tax

With the advent of massive online shopping, states are finally catching up to the opportunity to collect more sales tax. Stay on top of local initiatives in the jurisdictions where you operate.

Not only are people becoming more connected, but so are countries. They're beginning to share tax and revenue data in real time, in order to prevent companies from exploiting unintentional tax havens. We covered this more in Chapter 9. If you operate internationally, you must stay on top of tax developments continuously, or risk substantial fines.

Legal and regulatory

Hot topics include intellectual property decisions, who owns content, who controls internet access, etc. Not only are these issues continuously evolving, but they can differ dramatically around the globe in areas like data privacy and ownership.

Talent and reputation

We've all heard the stories of kids in garages creating the next hot app and retiring before they're old enough to drink. Just as athletes are being scouted in high school, major corporations are actively scouting and connecting with young, conspicuous talent. What are you doing to be aware of garage R&D in your industry?

Are you watching what's being said about your organization on Glassdoor.com and other sites? Do you have Google Alerts enabled so you find out at least as soon as your competitors do? (You should assume they have Google Alerts set up about you. You might think about reciprocating.) Attracting, retaining, developing, and leveraging talent can make or break an organization. New types of talent (digital, analytics, robotics) are critical to future growth, yet sometimes are not integrated into the pulse of the organization. Leveraged correctly, your talent is your best marketing engine; ignored or engaged only through one-way declarations, and your brand will drop precipitously.

7. *Where are organic and inorganic investment opportunities?*

Look at your strategic plan for the next few years, and go back to your plan from three years ago. Are the competitors the same? Are the key trends largely the same? If so, it's a good bet your business strategy may potentially be looking only at incremental effects versus transformational ones.

Is your organization viewing digital opportunities through each of the four lenses of Build versus Partner versus Invest versus Buy? Each has pros and cons as well as a potential role to tap into digital transformation opportunities. Many organizations think that Build is the solution to everything, believing that they know their business best and want to maintain control. Conversely, other companies use precious capital to buy companies without truly assessing the best way to integrate and drive step-function growth. The reality is that organizations need to begin by looking outside-in to determine the potential moves that will resonate, and then use the Build/Partner/Invest/Buy filter to determine the best way to proceed.

Feeling overwhelmed? Join the club. But there is a way forward

You may ask how you can possibly be expected to stay on top of all these areas and still run a business. We have the following three responses:

1. No one said it would be easy.
2. You don't need to sprint if you're not yet walking. The trick is first to make sure you're aggressively assessing these areas in your business, and taking the appropriate actions at some frequency; over time, this will become an integral part of the strategy and operations of the business.
3. You don't need to become expert at all of these areas when you can leverage trade associations, advisors, or other industry groups.

You may also think, "We're too small to have to worry about all these factors" or "this doesn't apply to us" for whatever reason.

It may be true that certain factors are currently not relevant. For example, you may not be doing business in other countries, or some emerging trends may not be as significant in your sector. Be careful not to let reasons such as these keep you from doing some serious thinking about your digital capabilities and transformation opportunities.

In EY's experience in more than 150 countries, these are the kinds of questions that modest-size (as well as large-scale) companies should be asking. In our digital world, these have become fundamental business questions in order to keep up, not to mention drive profitable growth. It's true that the scale of a smaller company is different, but the questions are not: Am I engaging with the customer? Am I paying attention to what my customer is now expecting from me, my competitors, and other industries? Am I operating efficiently? Am I improving my processes in order to maintain margins? These and the other questions we covered are all very much relevant to businesses of any meaningful size.

This is for certain

Earlier we talked about the continuum of phases 1.0, 2.0, and 3.0. Similarly, every business of every size has to make a decision about where and how it wishes to embrace the reality of business strategy in a digital world.

Option 1: Standing still

You risk being left behind by your customers.

Sure, some customers are friction-based. It's too much of a pain to move their business. But when a competitor does crack the code on making it easy for frustrated, sedentary customers to move, these standing-still businesses will find themselves in a digital sinkhole: the ground seemed solid, until it completely gave way.

Option 2: Grudgingly moving in reaction

These companies finally get moving, but seem to always be a few miles behind the curve. They use technology without any innovation. They're the ones with so-called brochure websites that are little more than online phone books. As customers, we encounter them every day, and are more than happy to leave them when anything better comes along.

Option 3: Becoming a fast follower

These companies keep an eye on the pioneers. They use technology quickly but with little innovation. A lot of money can be made this way, if the company is fast enough and has strong sales and delivery systems.

Then again, no one remembers the second person to fly across the Atlantic.

Option 4: Innovating

It's certainly a risk to be too early to the party. Jeff Bezos acknowledges a string of failed products that Amazon had high hopes for. However, the strongest companies look at failure as experiments to learn from.

There is the inevitable pushback by armchair sports fans who "knew it all along" that the product or service would fail. Then again, when the innovation does succeed, the company gets to enjoy the disproportionate attention that accompanies new products and services. In addition, early adopter customers are willing to pay a premium for bragging rights.

Is one option the best? No. But we submit that the companies adopting one of the first two options are destined to fight for the crumbs.

Get accustomed to the reality that we *all* need help. We can't build it on our own. We can't learn it all. Even the companies with the deepest pockets realize this, and don't try to grow all capabilities internally. They buy talent. Even then they have to make choices and not get into certain markets because they made the conscious decision to focus on other markets.

The key is to be regularly reviewing new information, and regularly making those conscious decisions instead of reactive moves. Make sure your company is reframing the question from "What is our digital strategy?" to "What is our business strategy in a digital world?"

NOTE

1. Anita Balakrishnan, "Jeff Bezos Plans to Get Millions of People to Space—and He's Selling $1 Billion a Year of Amazon Stock to Do iIt", CNBC, April 5, 2017, https://www.cnbc.com/2017/04/05/amazon-jeff-bezos-discusses-blue-origin-at-the-33rd-space-symposium.html.

13 | How can you pre-empt activist shareholders?

Shyam Gidumal

I was a shareholder activist.

At the time, that term hadn't yet been coined; however, the foundation had been set for a fundamental realignment in the way investors, boards, and management teams interacted.

I joined with a group of investors who owned stock in Vista 2000, Inc., a public company that had been a highflier on the NASDAQ. Unfortunately for them, management and the board had not succeeded in implementing the strategy they had promised. When the results fell short of projections, they cooked the books. The stock collapsed after questions were raised about the accuracy of prior financial statements.

I was the turnaround expert of the group. The more we dug, the worse the governance and malfeasance appeared to be. We engaged with the legacy board, which was largely populated by friends of the founder/CEO: a professional baseball team manager, an academic, the CEO's personal tax accountant, and so on. Eventually, after some tense discussions, we negotiated an arrangement to take control of the board. We filed a Form 8-K to make other investors aware of the reality we had uncovered.

The management team and board had failed on multiple fronts. Not only had the financials been inaccurate, but the company had liquidity issues—the banks had accelerated the loans. The company also had Regulation S toxic preferred securities outstanding and a variety of legal issues that needed to be addressed, including class action lawsuits. Underlying all of it were operational issues: most of their previous acquisitions were unprofitable, had not been integrated well, and were not operating effectively.

It was not enough for us to diagnose the problems; we needed solutions. I was elected president of the public company. We quickly fixed and then divested some of the businesses to pay down debt and calm the banks. We redeemed the Regulation S preferred stock and settled the class-action lawsuits. We then went to work making the remaining businesses profitable. We were eventually able to issue a set of audited financials. In the end, the company returned to being a stable public company that went on to generate positive shareholder value.

How activism has changed

The governance model of the postwar era stayed basically the same for 30 or 40 years. When a shareholder suggested that a company should change direction, the usual response from management could be summarized as: "If you don't like what I am doing, sell my stock."

Then in the early to mid-1980s, the leveraged buyout (LBO) boom changed the model (see Figure 13.1). Management said, "If you don't like what I am doing, sell my stock," and investors replied, "No, we'll just take you private and tell you what to do." This was the era recounted in books like *Barbarians at the Gate: The Fall of RJR Nabisco*[1] and *The Predators' Ball*.[2]

The story of Vista 2000, Inc. took place during this first phase: one-on-one activism. We were investors who directly interacted with a company. We were a stand-alone group, and our combined capital limited the size of the company we could engage.

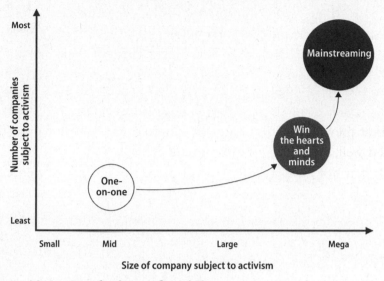

Figure 13.1 Evolution of activism

For that reason, large companies long believed that they were free from campaigns because activists couldn't raise enough money to take a sufficiently large stake to get standing.

The next phase began in the first decade of the twenty-first century. You can call it the "win the hearts and minds of institutional shareholders" phase. This new breed of activist engaged in a two-front war: first, the activist dealt directly with the company and had a conversation about what he or she thought should happen. The second front involved making presentations to institutional shareholders in order to elicit their support. Such shareholders own very large positions in the stock. In some highly publicized fights, the activist directly controlled only 1% or 2% of the stock, but ended up convincing enough institutional shareholders to support proposed changes that the company felt compelled to act.

During this time if a company said, "If you don't like what we're doing, sell our stock" (the first phase of activism), the new response was, "No, we will persuade other shareholders to support us and change the board of directors."

Now we are in the third phase of activism: mainstreaming. In get earlier incarnations, activists tended to be specialists. Often they were dedicated funds that focused the majority of their investing on companies from which they could generate higher returns by taking an active role. In this new phase we are seeing the growth come from occasional activists, who usually are traditional institutional investors that become active in specific situations.

Gone are the days where passive institutions had to call a specialist activist to promote their agenda. Now they can take the mantle by themselves.

Mainstreaming has had dramatic implications. It has expanded the investment theses that activists pursue. Historically, activists focused on whole company sales and balance sheet restructuring. Now the target's value improvement comes from business portfolio restructuring and operational improvements as well. This shift will continue to have dramatic effects on board composition, board-management interactions, and overall corporate governance.

Four areas of focus for activists

Here are the four types of investment theses that activists regularly pursue with companies:

1. Full company sale

Activists ask themselves: "Is there a public/private arbitrage on this company?" or "Might it be worth more to a strategic buyer?" For example, private equity and strategic investors might be currently buying companies for 12 times EBITDA. If your company is currently trading at 6 times EBITDA, your company will show up on their scans. Some of the earliest activist actions were putting a company in play. Activists have also been willing, at times, to be the buyer of the company, creating a tangible backstop for the existing shareholders.

2. Balance sheet restructuring, buybacks, and changes in dividend policy

The next questions activists often ask are: "What is the balance sheet position of this company? Is there an opportunity to increase debt and generate a big cash dividend that comes back to us? Are there other financing activities such as sale/leasebacks and factoring that can generate cash?"

Balance sheet restructurings have been a mainstay of activism from its earliest incarnations. They range from the plain vanilla—raise traditional debt and generate a buyback or dividend—to more complex structures. For example, in Pershing Square's investment in Target Corporation, a key element of the investment thesis it made public was the proposal for Target to spin off its owned land into a ground lease real estate investment trust (REIT) and thereby increase its leverage, and at the same time reduce its borrowing cost.

3. Business portfolio restructuring

Activists look at a multidivisional company and ask a question similar to the previous "full company sale" question, except now they ask themselves: "Can we create value by breaking up this company into two or three pieces?"

Many companies have addressed proposals to be split into parts: eBay/PayPal, PepsiCo, and DuPont, to name a few. Some have succeeded in convincing their shareholders that the benefit of keeping the pieces together exceeds the cost of having multiple parts, yet others have not.

4. Operational improvement

Activists study benchmarks in your industry and best-in-class industries, and then ask: "Is this company as a whole, or at a divisional level, exhibiting the right operational performance? If it improved operations, is there an opportunity to move the stock to another level? Is the company comparing itself to best-in-class or just to industry peers?"

Operational improvement demands have been growing faster than any other investment thesis. In 2010, they accounted for less than 10% of activist demands; by 2017 they were the primary demand in more than 40% of activist actions.

The best protection against activism

Your best protection against activism is to think through how you look to an activist and be able to answer the questions an activist would ask you—*in advance.*

Whether or not you accept our assertion that activism is latent in most companies and is here to stay, it is prudent to act as if you accept it. It's the same principle as buying homeowner insurance even though you don't expect a wide array of hazards to befall your property.

In the case of preparing for shareholder activism, the insurance premium you pay is to think deeply and regularly about your business from the perspective of outsiders. From a business-planning point of view, that is not a bad premium to pay.

You can't optimize what you don't focus on

It's important to recognize the substantial difference in focus and vocabulary between activists and most business leaders. Activists and private equity investors judge company performance through investment lenses, such as ROIC and balance sheet efficiency.

As we discussed in Chapter 8, senior executives of public companies tend to evaluate their businesses from the perspective of the income statement. They analyze return on sales and margins, but do not spend as much time on the balance sheet. This is especially true for multidivisional companies. They also generally benchmark within their sector, but rarely beyond it.

This difference in focus generates a disconnect when companies look at their world and conclude they are doing a good job because they've optimized their income statement compared to their industry peers. At the same time, activists look at your company through an ROIC lens, and may well conclude that the ROIC you're giving investors is not adequate, or that certain underutilized assets could be freed up. They may also be aware, for example, that a best-in-class supply chain resides in another industry, so there is room for substantial improvement in yours.

That is why the Capital Agenda is so crucial for companies to understand and thoroughly apply. One key principle of the Capital Agenda is to look at your company from other perspectives, especially the outside-in view of investors.

Activists review the potential stock improvement opportunities that result from their evaluations, and then determine the potential to act on those findings. For example, they may conclude that operational improvements could very well take a company to another level, but it will require capital investment.

They also look at their opportunity to effect the proposed changes. Activists have many tools at their disposal for persuading companies to make changes, including:

- Informal suggestions
- Precatory proposals (nonbinding proposals put to shareholders)
- Tender offers
- Proxy fights
- Litigation

The choice of tool will depend on the activists' experience with them, and the specific dynamics of the target company.

Boards must also change

Traditionally, the board hired a CEO, set overall strategy, and then judged whether the management team was doing a good job.

Now companies and boards are realizing that institutional investors want to have more exposure to the board members they elect(ed).

Investors want to get comfortable that the board in fact shares the same priorities that institutional investors think they should have.

Activists' deeper involvement into operational issues than in previous times, coupled with their expectation of greater access to board members, may change the skills that you need on your board. To be responsive to these institutional investors, boards must have the knowledge to get deeper into operational levers with the management team. They must be familiar with the investment theses outlined earlier, and with granular operational details along the lines of "What are best-in-class supply chain costs, and how do we get to that level?"

What to do when the activist's letter arrives

The most important thing to do first when an activist's letter arrives is not to think in "bad/good" or "defense/offense" binary terms, and certainly not to engage based on your gut reaction.

It's important to listen to what the activist has to say, and take enough time for a thoughtful response. That first communication back to the activist can set the stage for the many interactions to come. The tone must be right.

A little-known fact in activism is that when companies engage effectively during the initial encounters, the majority of activists come and go with no press headlines.

You can craft the right tone by working through the following questions:

What do you know about the activist's proposal?

The activist may be clear about the recommended course of action, or not. If it's the latter, then your first order of business should be to ask for elaboration or clarification of the activist's initial message. That very action can help to reduce tensions because it's respectful and constructive to ask for further information.

Be careful not to jump to conclusions about what you think is the endgame of the activist. Earlier we covered the four most common areas of focus, but of course there may be others. You are best served by engaging directly on the activist's topics without making assumptions or letting egos get in the way.

What can you find out about the experience and interaction style of the activist?

A great deal of information is available these days. Many activists have created a long public record of prior encounters. You can rapidly build a dossier of sorts on activists from that history. You can learn their prior tendencies, who has worked where, and who has been involved in what sort of activities. This process may not immediately provide clarity, but you are assembling information that may help you to see trends and also styles of behavior.

This is a good time to ask around in your network, and possibly enlist an advisor who may have a much larger network to query.

You may be looking at a positive situation if you determine that the activist is offering help in the form of directors or advisors who have successfully created value at other companies.

In your annual or quarterly reviews, have you anticipated the specific questions or comments now being made by the potential activist?

If you've been doing your stress testing effectively, there's a high likelihood that you already have information that addresses the issues raised by the activist. It might need a little updating, but it's in your playbook. Advisors can help you frame the information so it can be presented in order to best address the issue at hand.

Formulating your response

To maximize the chances of productive engagement with an activist, you need to be aware of the three components of an activist encounter:

- **Tactics and processes.** How should you navigate proxy solicitation rules, Section 220 demands for books and records inspection, etc?
- **Defensive facts.** What facts can you bring to bear to show the activist's arguments are mistaken or misguided?
- **Offensive measures.** How are you planning to generate shareholder returns? Why should the shareholders support management's plan?

In our experience, companies typically spend 90% to 95% of their energy around tactics and processes. They spend around 5% of their energy on true defense, and they spend almost no energy on offense or asserting why their vision and strategy are the right ones.

Why is this? Because historically the shareholder activist playbook was an offshoot of the hostile defense playbook, which traditional advisors typically used. That approach was somewhat effective during the early one-on-one phase, but is much less effective now that institutional shareholders are fully engaged.

Consider this high-profile example: a company had two divisions and an activist asserted that management would create shareholder value if the divisions were separated. Management disagreed and engaged in a long and expensive proxy fight. The company won the proxy battle, yet never settled suspicions in the investor base that the activist might have been right. Less than a year after winning the battle, management decided to separate the businesses. In the end, the company lost the war because it was so focused on the tactical/process steps that it failed to convince the investor base of its strategy.

In dealing with an activist, you will at some point also need to communicate with other shareholders, proxy advisors, and other interested parties about the activist's proposals. Shareholders generally care very little about tactics. Most investors do not care about the proxy rules in Delaware, strategies for bypassing the nominating committee, and other such details. They care about what will drive the stock in the long term.

A more realistic and effective mixture of the three factors is to spend your energy and resources as follows: 30% on tactics, 30% on defense, and 40% on offense. What shareholders really want to hear is the tangible ways in which your approach will enhance shareholder value. They want you to articulate how the activist's position is factually wrong—not in terms of general principles, but in terms of specific facts. The activist laid out quantitative facts and arguments, and shareholders want to see quantitative arguments from you around those very same specific topics.

We thought about that, too

The objective in your initial conversations with activists is to have them very quickly recognize that their idea is something that you in fact have already thought through. Ideally, the position you have and the actions you've taken are in line with their understanding of what's happening out there, not divergent from it or blind to it. Companies can be very successful in having activists come and go without drama and without board change, if those encounters with activists are handled in the way we propose.

As we advocated in Chapter 2, engage proactively with your institutional shareholders, and with your shareholders in general. Do this at least annually and possibly even quarterly, and between quarters as necessary. The communication should cover the following three areas:

1. Strategic decisions you've made
2. Unusual financial performance
3. Nonintuitive decisions, and your basis for making them

For example, if you have a division that is quite different from all your other divisions, explain the economic value in keeping it. Describe why that division should stay with the parent company, especially if you don't have any overlap in sales force, distribution, or marketing. Explain why it is strategically important for you to have those pieces together.

You should also be able to outline how, for example, you would have to write a big tax check if you were to sell off a division as the activist suggests, or what the economics of the transaction would look like if you were to do a sale/leaseback.

Describing your strategic thinking should be something you do with the marketplace on a regular basis, and not just when an activist shows up and says you should divest certain assets.

Finally, it's important to realize that the last thing an activist wants to do is get stuck in a bad investment. Let's say I'm an activist and think that the way I get 50% appreciation is by having you sell Division X for US$2 billion in cash. After I buy the stock and we fight with each other for a while, I learn that there's a US$1 billion tax bill that must be paid, and therefore you won't get US$2 billion in cash for it, but only US$1 billion. That is not good for my stock position, given that I'm now active and have taken a big position, filed a Form 13-D, and so on. It's nearly impossible for me to sell the stock without the price plummeting and handing me a poor return.

By anticipating activist questions and requests, and then addressing them quickly with facts and details, you allow activists to learn very early on that their thesis is flawed. They can quickly and quietly get out of the position before much is known about it, and you both can move on.

Activism is here to stay

Not only is activism not a fad, but it is becoming more pervasive by the year. It's not a question of whether you have activists in your shareholder base, but of when they might go from latent to active. It's not a matter of them finding you; you already have them. By taking the steps we describe, you will be in the best position to reduce or even head off any activist tendencies among your shareholders.

Notes

1. Bryan Burrough and John Helyar, *Barbarians at the Gate: The Fall of RJR Nabisco* (New York: Harper & Row, 1989).
2. Connie Bruck, *The Predators' Ball* (New York: Penguin, 1988).

14

How should you restore a distressed company to health?

Andrew Wollaston and Donald Featherstone

When economic waters are calm, it is hard to imagine the effect that financial disruption can have on an enterprise. A CEO and owner of a company borrowed to expand his business during profitable times. He believed that taking on debt had relatively low risk when compared to the equity returns that profits from expansion would deliver. Unfortunately, 12 months later a major annuity customer switched to a competitor and the company couldn't recover the lost revenue elsewhere. The CEO told us:

> On reflection, I should have taken immediate steps to cut costs and reshape the business for lower volumes, but I thought another major contract win was just around the corner. Anyway, the debt was three-year money, and I assumed the business was still making a profit.

After six months of negative cash flow, the business breached the terms of its lending agreement and had insufficient cash to make a debt payment. The lenders urgently requested a meeting and a proposal from the company on how to handle the situation. The business had developed a new product line, and the CEO was confident that market appetite was strong, although there were no actual sales in the pipeline. He asked the banks to increase their exposure to fund the company's future.

> *I see now that I was overly optimistic. The lenders asked all the right questions; unfortunately, I was not well prepared and did not have proper business plans, cash flow forecasts, and commercial due diligence to demonstrate why they should support the business. That also meant I had nothing to show other capital providers.*

Within two months, the business was on the verge of bankruptcy and its debt had been sold to other financial institutions—principally credit funds—which took a clinical view of the loan and demanded repayment. Through a consensual debt-for-equity swap, the funds took control of the business, put in a new management team, and subsequently funded a merger with a competitor.

> *I thought I was in control. It took me too long to realize I wasn't, and by then it was too late.*

Every restructuring situation starts as a healthy business with all the hopes of being successful. It is a complex process to return a business to viability after suffering through a period of financial and operational distress. Most restructurings are multidimensional and require a combination of capabilities, including strategic planning, stakeholder management, operational transformation, cash flow management, and M&A expertise—essentially every element of the Capital Agenda. In addition to bringing a diverse set of capabilities together, restructuring increasingly involves an international legal dimension. Legal regimes in developed economies differ, sometimes significantly, in how to address corporate rehabilitation. Understanding the options, strategies, and pitfalls of one restructuring regime versus another requires broad knowledge of multiple legal systems and their relative merits in a particular situation. All of these factors converge to create a rich but complex environment for restoring corporate health—once described as akin to playing chess on a three-dimensional board.

The intricacies of restructuring affect each company in a unique way. However, successful restructuring processes have a common set of characteristics. These include:

- Understanding the nature of operational turnarounds versus financial restructurings.
- A recognition of how to manage the human dimension of corporate distress.
- A plan for marshaling recovery.
- The ability to maintain control of the situation.

We discuss each in turn below.

Turnaround versus restructuring

The term *restructuring* is used in a variety of ways to describe how a company deals with financial and operational distress. In some contexts, the term is interchangeable with *turnaround* and *transformation*. However, it is important to use precise definitions because turnarounds and restructurings are distinct concepts.

Turnaround

A turnaround generally refers to improving and restoring a company's profitability and cash flow. Turnaround can equally apply to a healthy company making changes to an underperforming division, and to a distressed company urgently looking to improve its cash flow. A turnaround can be limited in scope or include sweeping changes to the enterprise. Public companies often refer to turnaround activities as a transformation program because the term *transformation* has a slightly more affirmative ring to it. Figure 14.1 shows concrete examples of turnaround activities.

Category	Examples
Revenue and gross margin improvement	Customer profitability, cost to serve various customer segments, pricing, expansion into adjacent markets
Production cost reduction	Footprint optimization, outsourcing, machine efficiency
Overhead and administrative cost reduction	Functional efficiencies, shared service models, elimination of duplicate functions
Working capital and cash flow optimization	Inventory management, supply chain restructuring (see Chapter 8)
Portfolio optimization via divestments	Disposal of poorly performing units (see Chapters 4 and 6)
Human capital and organizational design changes	Changing from a divisional structure to a product-line structure

Figure 14.1　Turnaround activities

Turnarounds focus on increasing the overall enterprise value of a company but do not usually address how a company's value is allocated to stakeholders.

Restructuring

Restructuring refers to a realignment of the debt and equity claims on a company's enterprise value. It deals with the important issues of how much debt and equity a company has, the priority of creditors' claims, and the manner in which various stakeholders bear the consequences of distress. Most European restructurings are done consensually, meaning stakeholders must generally perceive any allocation of value to be reasonable and fair. There are also times when a consensual restructuring cannot be organized and a legal process must take place to help ensure the equitable allocation of value. This is particularly common when there are holdout creditors or the requisite level of consent cannot be obtained to implement a consensual arrangement. A few examples of restructuring actions are:

- Seeking waivers and amendments to credit facilities.
- Rescheduling interest and amortization payments.
- Swapping debt for equity.
- Negotiating consensual agreements among creditors.
- Using legal processes like Chapter 11 in the United States or various schemes or arrangements in common law regimes.
- Liquidating some or all of a business.

Although we describe turnarounds and restructurings as separate concepts, in practice they are highly interdependent and both are usually required to fully rehabilitate a distressed company. Very few businesses enter distress simply owing to their capital structure; usually an underlying set of causes propels a company toward underperformance. These can include technological disruption, currency or commodity price shocks, changes to the competitive landscape, or political events.

Recognizing corporate distress and the human dimension

The first step on the path to recovery is coming to grips with the psychological effect of corporate distress.

Though no two restructurings are identical, most go through certain general phases, with the details differing from one company to the next. These phases have consequences on many different levels: some are apparent in financial and operational performance; others are more subtle and play out on a psychological level. Let's look at the seven general phases of corporate distress:

Phase 1. The seed of a problem becomes apparent to management, even though they may not verbalize it or take action.

Phase 2. The problem grows, while being rationalized away. This phase can last for weeks or years, depending on how well capitalized the company is, and whether performance in some units serves to mask underperformance elsewhere.

Phase 3. Cash resources begin to dwindle as problems persist.

Phase 4. The cash crisis drives management to realize that something radically different needs to be done, and it is no longer business as usual.

Phase 5. The board and outside accountants recognize going-concern issues. In other words, after reviewing the financials, they're forced to reveal that the viability of the business as a going concern is in doubt. Debt covenant breaches may also trigger this result.

Phase 6. Creditors and lawyers get together and begin to dictate—not suggest—terms by which the company must now operate.

Phase 7. By this late phase, management's options depend on the specific circumstances. Next steps could include divestments, recapitalization, management changes, or liquidation of the company.

Many businesses are born, live, and die without any effort at rehabilitation. When businesses do need help, it is a regrettable fact of the turnaround profession that practitioners generally get called in during the later phases of the process. Though there are many reasons for this, it usually comes down to a need to overcome psychological inertia around recognizing difficult times. Corporate distress is a form of loss and, like any form of loss, the human mind has certain defense mechanisms that may or may not help the situation.

In the face of distress, people often are overly optimistic about future results and the ability to achieve them. In many cases, executives may realize they have a problem and even that they're ill-equipped to deal with it. However, they don't seek expert assistance because they worry that the very act of doing so will trigger even more problems. Some companies may seek assistance in phase 3 when cash is short. On the other hand, because cash is short, they may assume that they cannot cover regular expenses, much less afford experienced restructuring talent. All of these are symptoms of the need to come to grips with the reality of the situation and what can be done about the loss associated with the decline of business.

For both senior executives and restructuring practitioners, being sensitive to the human dimension of corporate distress is a prerequisite to being effective. Though it is important to be decisive during difficult times, traditional leadership models of command and control rarely get the best out of an organization. Even in midsize companies, a team of restructuring professionals will constitute only a small portion of the available management resources. One of the critical balancing acts of any successful restructuring process is to find ways to identify with and motivate a larger management team while remaining disciplined about results.

A key element of this balancing act involves understanding the difference between management and leadership. Management is generally about maintaining the status quo. Leadership, in contrast, is about motivating change. A company that needs to change in order to survive requires clear leadership. Part of the leadership challenge of a turnaround or restructuring involves getting a management team to willingly adopt new ways of working. Among other things, this involves projecting a positive vision of the future, measuring and celebrating successes, and rewarding positive outcomes. The conventional notion of restructuring as a negative activity is completely at odds with the reality of how corporate health is restored. The job of senior executives and restructuring practitioners is to define the "finest hour" for the organization and to direct everyone's energies to the most important objectives.

Marshaling the recovery

Successful corporate rehabilitation almost always involves both an operational turnaround and a financial restructuring. Problems usually are specific to culture, operating model, market position, and financial strength. Despite these challenges, stakeholders will agree to a restructuring only when they are confident that a company's plan to maximize enterprise value will be executed successfully.

Leading a campaign to restore corporate health involves addressing six critical turnaround and restructuring activities. These points are listed roughly in the order in which they should be addressed, but in practice many must be managed in parallel.

1. Establish and maintain stability.
2. Diagnose what needs to be fixed.
3. Formulate a compelling and actionable turnaround strategy.
4. Adapt the capital structure to realistic cash flow forecasts.
5. Build implementation around clear leadership and operational discipline.
6. Communicate openly with external and internal stakeholders.

1. Establish and maintain stability

A company and its stakeholders need financial and operational stability to be able to assess the situation and formulate strategies for a successful turnaround and restructuring. Stability has two related components: time and liquidity.

In many cases, additional time can be provided via a standstill agreement or similar mechanism whereby external stakeholders agree not to enforce their rights and remedies. Additional time early on provides all parties the opportunity to evaluate the company and their own positions in order to prepare for later stages of the financial restructuring process.

Stability also requires that the company have sufficient liquidity to operate. There is little value to undertaking a broad operational turnaround program only to run out of cash halfway through the process. Liquidity is the lifeblood of a company, because management must meet its critical commitments to employees, vendors, and other parties who are essential to maintaining operational stability. Short-term liquidity can sometimes be accomplished through working capital improvement initiatives. See Chapter 8. However, many companies have exhausted self-help measures by the time they enter discussions with stakeholders, and require some form of outside liquidity support. In practice, liquidity is often provided by supersenior facilities or by pledging collateral that is not encumbered by other creditors.

2. Diagnose what needs to be fixed

With a degree of stability in place, management needs a clear, concise understanding of what needs to be fixed. A rigorous diagnosis builds stakeholders' confidence that the company knows what actions need to be taken to restore value. In some cases, it is useful to look back in time to when an enterprise was profitable and formulate a bridge to the present in order to see in clear relief what revenue and cost items have changed. Figure 14.2 provides an example of an EBITDA bridge.

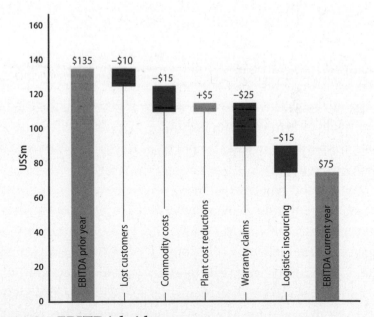

Figure 14.2   EBITDA bridge

Boiling down the diagnosis to a few key causal factors early in the process helps focus turnaround execution efforts later on, and provides an explanation to stakeholders unfamiliar with the details of a company's operations.

3. Formulate a compelling and actionable turnaround strategy

With a clear sense of what needs to be fixed, management is better prepared to formulate strategies for rehabilitation. Turnaround strategies are different from the conceptual approaches that have been institutionalized by some consulting firms. The turnaround plan needs to be credible and achievable because stakeholders will spend a great deal of effort scrutinizing each detail, especially in contested situations. Turnaround strategies usually focus on initiatives within the company's control like cost reduction, disposal of underperforming operations, and governance changes. Initiatives that rely on outside parties like revenue growth, increasing market share, and renewed marketing programs are important, but much less persuasive when negotiating with stakeholders.

4. Adapt the capital structure to realistic cash flow forecasts

With a compelling operational turnaround plan underway, it is now time to turn to the financial restructuring. Once a management team has an achievable projection of future cash flows, it is in a strong position to engage with stakeholders to develop a sustainable capital structure that supports the company's turnaround efforts.

Leverage negotiations often veer into discussions about EBITDA multiples or other similar high-level metrics. Multiples can be highly misleading and fail to take into account important items like capital expenditures, restructuring costs, and accumulated trade liabilities. By staying focused on the details of expected future cash flows, a company is more likely to arrive at a capital structure it can afford over the long term. It is also less likely to encounter the cumbersome task of returning to the restructuring process shortly after concluding negotiations with stakeholders. Well-constructed cash flows also include stress testing to highlight how well the capital structure could withstand temporary shortfalls from the base-case forecasts.

5. Build implementation around clear leadership and operational discipline

General George Patton once said, "A good solution applied with vigor now is better than a perfect solution applied 10 minutes later." Execution is one of the most underrated parts of operational turnaround and financial restructuring processes. Urgently following through on commitments to change is essential to restoring value and generating trust with stakeholders. Implementation requires good governance and strong operational discipline. The management team must carefully select metrics, manage trade-offs among competing objectives, and assign accountability for delivering results.

Leading practices for implementation include:

- Gaining commitment from the board and executive leadership.
- Clearly communicating objectives and milestones to operational management.
- Monitoring results weekly with reporting to both executive and operational management.
- Making decisions quickly but deliberately.
- Celebrating successes throughout the process.

6. Communicate openly with external and internal stakeholders

Communication is one of the most neglected parts of turnaround and restructuring initiatives. It is a normal human reaction for a management team to withdraw into its own problems when faced with significant operational or financial distress. However, successful rehabilitation thrives on candid and frequent communication among management and stakeholders, including share owners, customers, suppliers, and employees.

Management needs to be open and fair in sharing information from the outset, so stakeholders can assess their own situations in order to agree to any restructuring of debt or equity claims. Without transparency, creditors in particular tend to assume the worst and may look to formal legal remedies to assert influence over the company.

Robust communication from the highest levels of leadership has a powerful influence on motivating staff, securing positive changes in culture, and maintaining a cadence for change. Over the longer term, regular communications celebrating interim achievements help to reinforce needed behavioral changes.

Remaining in control

Restructuring and turnaround competencies are built not just by mastering certain functional skills, but also by mastering specific situations while working in difficult conditions over many years. These holistic experiences are needed to address critical challenges promptly and to create confidence among employees, shareholders, creditors, and other stakeholders whose support is essential for a successful outcome. For example, lenders and other creditors in particular must be convinced the company understands the scope of the challenges ahead and that management's expectations for an achievable outcome are thoughtful and realistic.

With individual elements of the Capital Agenda, it's common for a company to undertake actions on its own initiative. With sufficient resources and experience, a company can build a strong M&A department, or become quite skilled in working capital optimization, tax structuring, or other important capabilities. However, because of its multidisciplinary demands, compressed time frames, and infrequency, restructuring is altogether a different endeavor, requiring a nearly simultaneous application of the entire Capital Agenda.

An advisor's independent views on how distress affects a company from a financial, operational, and human perspective are critical during all phases of a restructuring. Marrying this understanding with a knowledge of how various external stakeholders respond to corporate distress is invaluable when executives are navigating the difficult waters of a complex restructuring for the first time.

Turning around a company while wrangling a diverse set of external stakeholders is an extraordinary task, even for the most skilled management team. Employing independent help, such as a chief restructuring officer, to coordinate the restructuring process enables senior management to focus on the day-to-day business. This provides the space to pursue new business opportunities, develop new markets, and reinvigorate the company while turnaround and restructuring actions are advanced by a professional with experience in urgent corporate change. A single point of accountability also helps to ensure that the restructuring effort receives the necessary level of senior attention.

Time is of the essence

Many businesses with normal challenges measure time in yearly budgets, quarterly reports, and monthly quotas. A business recovering from financial distress must operate in sprints of weeks, weekends, days, and sometimes hours.

With the right approach backed by a deep bench, it's possible to accomplish an astonishing amount of work in a short period. Albeit on an abbreviated basis, over the course of a few short weeks a skilled professional working with an ambitious senior management team can conduct due diligence and produce a sound valuation, build complex models with which to test financing options and operational scenarios, and explore the possibility of mergers and divestments.

A few examples of urgent change include an American retailer that was able to diagnose its cost base and consolidate half of its distribution centers over the course of eight weeks. A Dutch offshore-services company reduced its overhead costs by 55% in 90 days, including the cumbersome process of consulting with labor unions. A UK manufacturing company was able to divest an underperforming division, negotiate a new pension arrangement, and refinance its debt—all over the course of a few months.

Exactly what can be accomplished quickly is often a heated topic with business leaders facing the need to restructure. With the right approach, it is possible to secure short-term creditor support based on informal discussions and to stand down threats of legal enforcement. These extraordinary actions are possible when time is of the essence and when the company and its advisors work together as a team.

Moving quickly can be disconcerting for highly data-driven companies that have a culture of decision making based on a comprehensive command of the facts. There are times during restructurings where full information is a luxury that neither a company nor its stakeholders can afford. Decisive action with a 60% level of confidence is often a better path than a more contemplative approach taken over time.

Traditional planning cycles need to be replaced by quick calls, impromptu meetings, and tentative agreements. Though the fast pace is often uncomfortable, it is absolutely necessary for a successful restructuring.

Liquidity is a moving target

In early discussions on cash flows it is critical to have an achievable view of projected receipts and disbursements. There is a tendency to assume debtors will pay early and creditors will allow payment on extended terms, even though financial distress is apparent.

In reality, when businesses get into trouble, it's soon on social media by employees who speculate that something is not right. Then it gets picked up by trade suppliers and customers. Before long, financial performance declines when customers stop paying (because they don't think they have to), and suppliers stop supplying.

Countering this crunch requires both transparency and detail in terms of where the cash will come from, and when. Businesses typically create monthly cash flow projections; we instead create a week-by-week projection for 13 weeks to enable granular and focused discussions with creditors and other stakeholders.

Don't close off options

No company anticipates needing an urgent restructuring. Management may have worked several options for recapitalizing the company, improving operations, or both. For whatever reason, these efforts were not successful and then the reality of limited liquidity started to close in.

What typically happens next is leadership goes from being optimists to pessimists in short order. Once cash runs out, their sincere but unsuccessful efforts can cause the organization to see only darkness ahead.

However, in practice there is rarely ever just one option. A well-orchestrated restructuring process can create options that aren't apparent at the start. Creditors often become willing to negotiate from a previous position of intransigence when presented with facts that clarify their true options and position.

One key tool in any restructuring is a stakeholder map, which is an overview of all the parties—suppliers, customers, employees, shareholders, and debt providers—along with their repayment priority and potential magnitude of loss. Figure 14.3 shows how the estimated value of the company aligns against the secured and unsecured claims. Where there are "value breaks" within the capital structure is a critical component to understanding the position of various stakeholders, their likely reaction to a restructuring proposal, and their ability to contribute new capital. In this basic example, the value break is at the subordinated notes. Assuming an enterprise value for this company of US$200 million—represented by the vertical arrow—only the senior debt has a good chance of being repaid in full.

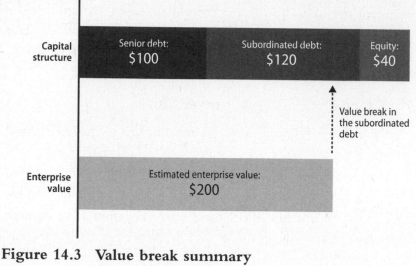

Figure 14.3   Value break summary
Note: Figures in US$m.

Sometimes so many stakeholders stand to lose so much—like the subordinated debtholders in Figure 14.3—that they're willing to work through a solution. This is especially true when many creditors rank side by side, so they all stand to lose a lot. It's not unusual for every bank, subcontractor, and employee to realize they can expect only 2 or 3 cents on the dollar if the current trajectory runs its course and the company fails.

Complex restructurings involve multiple stakeholders who have lent to, or who have equity interests in, different companies within a group. In cases like this, an entity priority model can illustrate returns under different scenarios and valuations. This model shows which stakeholders have a financial interest and those who may be out of the money. It provides an economic framework for negotiations and can support proposals in both consensual and court-driven restructuring processes.

With the right mix of interventions, businesses can often be financially restructured on a sixpence. Those actions include developing an unvarnished and comprehensive stakeholder map, coupled with a strategic plan that paints a realistic vision for the future. Senior management must be credible and communicate very crisply on the planned route through the current situation, and answer difficult questions about what the company will look like post-restructuring.

Early detection is the best prevention

As good as a successful restructuring can be, it is even better to avoid the precipice altogether. What are some ways to do that?

Businesses rarely get into profound trouble overnight. It's possible to find the occasional situation where product prices crater and a sudden liquidity emergency arises. Even then, creditors often have enough perspective to know that businesses with sudden drops in pricing are the same ones that can enjoy a sudden jump. Those types of situations involve financial restructurings that can often be worked out.

In contrast, we see financial distress caused by structural problems that go well beyond temporary price volatility. In retrospect, they often could have been detected many years earlier.

Take a major industrial company as an example, where a young engineer invented not a mere line extension but a radically new technology. Though the company earned royalties from patents on the technology, it did not seem to value its own disruptive invention as much as the marketplace did. A number of years later, the company found itself in major financial trouble, as its core business continued to erode in the wake of competitors making the most of that technology. Although the company stabilized its decline and continues to exist, one wonders what could have been.

It would have taken an exceptionally strong and persuasive leader to argue for increased investment in a disruptive technology that had the potential to destroy the company's main business. As part of a regular stress test, senior executives should have tasked a small group with articulating and constantly refreshing ways to maintain a market-leading position in the main business versus other technologies.

Whether disruption affects the whole company or an underperforming business unit, most CEOs usually have a reasonably honed instinct that something is wrong. They sense it fairly early on but rarely react to it. Maybe it's due to ego, or to the fear of having something fail on their watch; either way, when your gut tells you that you've got a problem—even though you think you're on top of it—it's important to get a third-party perspective.

Remaining in control requires early detection and decisive action. In our experience, the longer problems go unaddressed, the narrower the company-controlled solutions become. Once those options evaporate, creditors will dictate the outcome.

CEOs remark to us that it has become increasingly challenging to operate in an environment of lower growth, greater global competition, pop-up competitors with lean, digitally driven business models, sector and commodity price dislocations, and more activism in the equity and debt capital markets. Speed and agility have become fundamental to attaining and preserving competitive advantage See Chapter 10.

These same qualities drive successful turnarounds and restructurings. A company can remain in control of the process, manage external stakeholders, and maximize its options if it promptly identifies underperformance and solicits outside perspectives. The path to recovery is difficult, but with the right combination of experience, fortitude, understanding, and luck, there is almost always a brighter way forward.

15

Will your strategic goals ensure your company reaches its full potential?

Bill Achtmeyer and John Trustman

Throughout this book, strategy has been an ever-present and close partner of the Capital Agenda, but it hasn't had to work very hard. With the exception of our discussion of integrating strategy, finance, and operations (Chapter 10) and our deep dive into business strategy in a digital world (Chapter 12), we generally took for granted that a company's strategy was well-defined, value-creating, and properly connected with the rest of the enterprise. In reality, your Capital Agenda needs some heavy lifting from your strategy to fully answer questions like these:

- *Portfolio optimization.* Which of our businesses should we continue to own? Which should we divest? What gaps do we need to fill through building, buying, or partnering?
- *Capital allocation.* How much should we invest organically in each of our businesses? What can we afford to pay for acquisitions?

217

- *Valuation.* Which of these alternatives do investors favor? What strategic moves could increase our intrinsic value and market value, and reduce the gap between them?

Neither your Capital Agenda nor your strategy can be determined independently of the other. In Chapter 1 we defined the Capital Agenda as a comprehensive approach to managing capital, executing transactions, and applying practical corporate finance tools to strategic and operational decisions. Capital can't be allocated properly and the right transactions won't be executed until strategic decisions are made, including deciding which markets to operate in and how to best serve customers. And strategic alternatives need to be evaluated with the financially disciplined mindset and tools we discussed in Chapters 2 and 3.

To highlight the kinds of rigorous analyses you can perform to help make those strategic decisions, we're going to share a diagnostic tool kit we call the Full Potential Paradigm™ (FPP). FPP works with your Capital Agenda to assist in setting operational targets, informing portfolio strategy, and understanding investors' value drivers. Let's start with a short story.

A well-known media company was once a Wall Street darling, growing at 14% annually, based on both overall market growth and taking market share from the competition. But its focus on gaining share led to saturating the addressable market. Growth began to level out as the company reached what management viewed as its full potential.

When the next recession arrived, its market value declined dramatically, as negative GDP growth compounded its market saturation. The company could have followed several strategic initiatives to avoid such a hard hit from the market. It could have taken a more holistic perspective on setting targets, such as improving margins and investing in new services, or acquiring businesses with compelling synergies. The company could also have communicated better with investors to describe how it was reaching a more mature phase of growth that would better align with the market. These actions could have moderated investor expectations, and the market's reaction to the downturn might not have been so dramatic. In the pages ahead we'll describe a structured approach management could have followed.

A good strategy starts with setting the right targets

Reaching your company's full potential involves understanding the various paths to maximizing value, and starts with setting a data-driven strategy built on a robust Capital Agenda. One of your most important roles as a business leader is to establish realistic and achievable goals to guide decisions around choosing what markets to compete in and how. You need to identify and set these targets through a fact-based approach to analyzing what levels of profitable growth and sustainable margins are achievable. This effort employs certain universal concepts—such as business definition, relative market share (RMS), and competitive dynamics—that are relevant across industries and companies of all sizes.

FPP is a proprietary framework with four complementary elements that help illuminate part of the "Which targets should we set?" question:

1. Market context:
   ○ Have I properly defined my business, and do I understand the overall market and industry?
   ○ Do I understand the drivers of growth and profitability?
2. Margin performance:
   ○ Is my current business performing at its full potential?
   ○ Are the targets I am setting achievable and optimal for enabling the business to reach and sustain its full potential?
3. Growth opportunities:
   ○ Are our resources and targets aligned to maximize revenue and profit growth for the business?
4. Investor alignment:
   ○ Am I receiving appropriate recognition from investors for my company's accomplishments? Are market value and intrinsic value aligned?
   ○ Do I understand the capital markets' expectations for my business?

In today's dynamic and disruptive competitive environment, what CEO doesn't need to know the answers to these questions? And what CEO has solid quantitative answers to these questions in which he or she has a high level of confidence?

To set the stage, it is important to understand that FPP is based on what we call *maniacal realism*. This term represents our commitment to questioning assumptions and conventional wisdom in search of driving insights about a business.

Defining market context

Defining market context is a critical first step to help ensure your strategic goals fit your business and industry. This exercise identifies the specific industry and competitors, as well as growth and profit-ability drivers, and answers these questions:

- Is the industry consolidated or fragmented? Is it consolidating, fragmenting, or stable?
- What is the basis for competition?
- Where are the boundaries of your industry under attack?
- What are competitors' market shares, and how are they changing?

Defining your business is often not as straightforward as it sounds, given all the transformation and disruption in the world today. As an example of how complicated things can get: historically, Yellow Cab competed with Checker Taxi and other taxi companies. Today, it also competes with Uber and Lyft. Uber, in turn, is also competing with Amazon (in distribution) and car manufacturers (for transportation solutions). Does that mean Yellow Cab is competing with Amazon, Ford, Toyota, and General Motors?

Business definition takes into account both your business today and where it is headed, starting with a clean slate and not relying on conventional assumptions. The analysis looks at customers, competitors, and costs to identify peers and competitors. Understanding the value chain remains the core requirement, even though value chains have become increasingly complex, shared and digitized.

Mapping your market

An important first step is to create a Market Map of your business's position within its industry that shows individual companies' participation across segments, as well as the level and type of competition. Figure 15.1 maps the global beauty market at a recent point in time and shows the breakout of total industry sales by segment: skin care, hair care, cosmetics, and fragrances. Along the vertical axis are the individual market participants within each segment as a percentage of revenue. Each box on the chart represents a competitor's revenue in a segment.

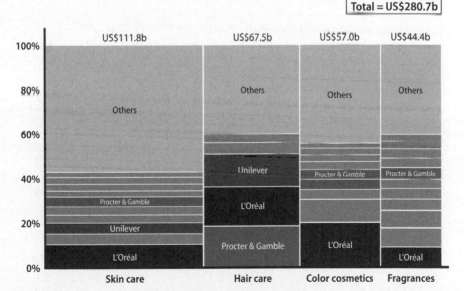

Figure 15.1 Global beauty Market Map.
Note: Companies with <2% market share in a given category are grouped into "Others." P&G's sales include beauty business sold to Coty in late 2016.
Source: EY analysis; Euromonitor.

We can make specific observations and formulate questions to help advance the analysis:

- Does segment market share appear to correlate with profitability?
- Are there smaller competitors that have good profitability? Why?
- What are the benefits of playing in multiple segments?
- Which acquisitions and segment divestments could create the most value?

Further segmenting the market (such as by geography or by men's and women's beauty/grooming) might generate more actionable insights. A full FPP process would determine what level of detail is sufficient, and in practice we suggest continuing until the story doesn't change.

Setting margin targets using the Performance Gap

A Performance Gap analysis examines a company's market position to help develop a rigorous understanding of achievable margins, and alternative paths for reaching them. On the way to setting operating margin targets that are aspirational but achievable, you should be able to answer these questions:

- How is profitability driven by our market position?
- Does being a market leader limit our profitability?
- How do we determine if our performance is sustainable?

For a properly defined business, profitability is driven by RMS,[1] so companies with high RMS should, all else being equal, earn more than those with lower RMS. This is derived from and similar to the experience curve.[2] Our research spanning more than 30 years shows that this relationship holds for both cost efficiencies and pricing advantage. In fact, high RMS does not tend to limit revenue growth, which debunks the notion that companies may be "too big to grow."

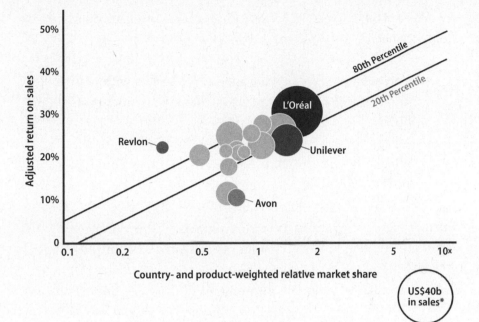

Figure 15.2   Global beauty Normative Band.
*This bubble area = US$40b in sales.
Source: EY analysis; Capital IQ; Euromonitor; analyst reports; company presentations.

Figure 15.2 is a diagnostic tool we call the Normative Band, which highlights where a company's profitability is on track, outperforming, or in need of improvement. Here we continue to look at the global beauty retail market. These concepts underpin the analysis:

- On the horizontal axis, RMS translates individual company market shares to show who in the industry has the most power.
- The vertical axis plots return on sales (ROS) adjusted for non-operating measures.
- The relationship of RMS to ROS follows the experience curve: profitability should improve by a repeatable fixed percentage over time for each doubling in RMS. In this example, we see how L'Oréal presents the highest RMS and, as a result, the highest profitability.

- The upper and lower bands (parallel diagonal lines) are relative performance indicators among competitors. We analyzed company data in more than 500,000 observations across several hundred industries. Consistently, exceptional performers usually perform at about the 80th percentile, which is where we draw the top of the Normative Band. Companies in the 80th percentile tend to stay around the 80th percentile with much greater stability than at any other performance level above the median. That makes the 80th percentile a great target because it's stable outperformance but not overperformance. Similarly, competitors falling below the 20th percentile (represented by the bottom of the Normative Band) tend not to recover.

Again, this analysis helps you develop useful hypotheses and questions about both the general market and specific companies, including:

- The first thing you notice is that the firms are highly clustered between 0.5 RMS and 2 RMS, and only one competitor is above the 80% band—the optimal performance. In other words, there are many players with middling margins, indicating a market that may be unstable and ripe for M&A—driven consolidation.
- Further analysis would be required to determine why Revlon is able to have significantly higher margins at significantly lower RMS.
- Is Avon's profitability low because of the cost of direct selling?

Based on where your company lies relative to the Normative Band (between the 20th and 80th percentile lines), there are multiple levers you could pull to reposition by moving up (more profitability) and to the right (greater market share). These potential strategies include acquisitions, divestments, and operational improvements to help achieve sustainable margins.

Setting growth targets with the Opportunity Gap

Where the Performance Gap focuses on business as it is today, the Opportunity Gap analysis shifts that focus to what could be—asking managers to look outside the box, albeit not necessarily very far outside, and often in someone else's box. The analysis works by identifying strategic opportunities that require further organic investment, while also identifying M&A and divestment prospects.

This analysis helps answer the following questions that are central to your Capital Agenda, particularly resource allocation and transaction execution:

- Am I over- or underinvesting in any of my businesses?
- Which of my businesses would benefit most from M&A?
- Are there businesses within my portfolio that are divestments candidates?

The Opportunity Strength Matrix (OSM) compares a business's strategic position to the opportunities available to that business. The notion of comparing strategic position to opportunity is as old as strategy consulting itself. The OSM builds on perhaps the best-known chart in strategy consulting, Boston Consulting Group's venerable Growth Share Matrix,[3] which uses a business segment's growth rate as a proxy for its opportunity. Now, decades later, companies can access much richer sources of information and sophisticated analytical tools to better assess market opportunity.

The OSM example in Figure 15.3 replaces the growth rate with a more predictive, industry-specific "opportunity attractiveness." Among the factors that can now be incorporated:

- Industry maturity based on adoption curves.
- Investment flows in converging industries that may be early indicators of disruption.
- Geographic segments with premium price points—for example, in consumer products.

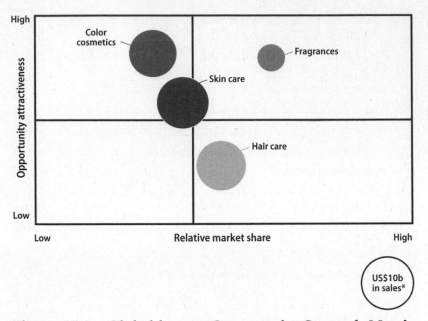

Figure 15.3   Global beauty Opportunity Strength Matrix.
Note: Illustrative example; does not represent an OSM for an actual industry participant.

Figure 15.3 shows that color cosmetics appears as both a current strong competitor and an interesting growth investment. Interestingly, in a traditional growth share matrix, color cosmetics would be least attractive based on its historical growth rate. Conversely, the hair care segment is clearly the least attractive based on the OSM analysis, though its growth rate would be equivalent to the other three businesses.

Aligning with investors via the Perception Gap

The Perception Gap uses regression models to deconstruct a company's market valuation to help align operating targets with investors' perspectives. Market participants rarely reveal all the factors that go into their stock valuations, so this analysis enables management to prioritize resource allocation and deploy capital more in sync with investor priorities. For example, if the company could improve both revenue and margin, but the Perception Gap analysis suggests that margin is a more important market value driver, then that's where management should focus more of its efforts.

The Perception Gap part of the FPP diagnostic supports answers to the following questions:

- Which controllable variables influence market value?
- What is the relative effect on valuation of each of these variables?
- Are our communications with the market in line with expectations and our performance?

Figure 15.4 summarizes a Market Value Drivers analysis looking at various contributions to a company's market capitalization.

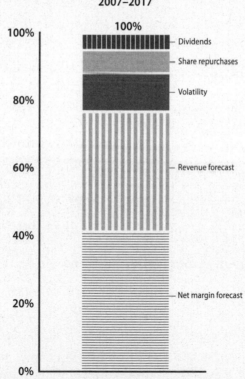

Figure 15.4 Market Value Drivers analysis
Source: EY analysis; Capital IQ; Oxford Economics.

Underlying the calculations is a sophisticated regression model that incorporates both company-specific and industry-wide variables.

Based on these results, if you were a board member or CEO, you would recognize that growth has historically been highly valued by the marketplace in the form of either revenue or margin over the long run. Therefore, assuming the same relationships hold into the future, focusing on shareholder payouts over profitable growth would not maximize value.

Full potential value synthesis

Once the business definition is complete and tested, base and stretch targets are established, and we have a core understanding of the drivers of market valuation and investor expectations, we start to model various scenarios for achieving full potential. These strategic options might include anything from incremental improvements to new market entry and to transformative acquisitions and divestments.

Figure 15.5 presents one scenario that examines the effects of two acquisitions on a company. Starting in the lower left and reading the chart from left to right, we can understand:

- How the company expects to grow on a stand-alone basis through 2020.
- The disproportionate effect of acquisition A, which would rely heavily on the acquiring company to improve margins, versus acquisition B, where margins would not be an issue.

Then reading up the chart, we see the remaining margin improvement necessary to reach the combined company's full potential value by achieving the 80th percentile in its Normative Band.

By pulling together all four FPP components and visually comparing alternatives, management can explore different combinations of organic initiatives and the sequencing of possible acquisitions and divestments.

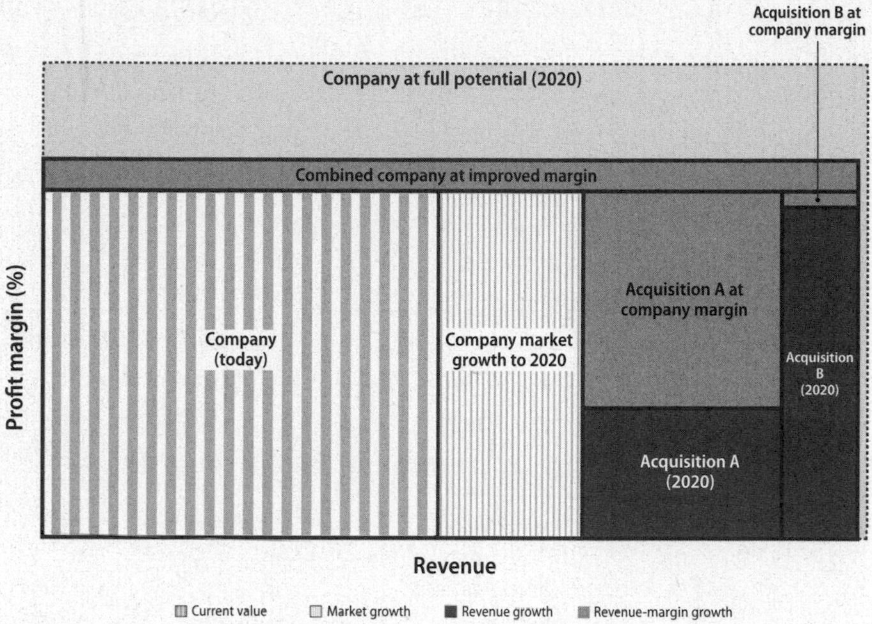

Figure 15.5 Full potential value synthesis

In this brief tour of the FPP diagnostic, we've seen how detailed and focused analytics help support strategic choices about which markets to invest in and which to exit. Integrating and qualifying these insights with a robust Capital Agenda helps provide actionable perspectives on capital allocation, portfolio optimization, and investor communications.

■ ■ ■

We've given you a tremendous amount of material within these 15 chapters that distills many careers' worth of insights and experiences. We don't expect that all of it applies to you or that you'll be able to act on all of it at once. But you are in the enviable position of being able to choose where your initial 5% improvement comes from (see Chapter 1). Then you can celebrate, go for another 5%, and another, and soon you'll be creating value and building resilience, and widening the gap between you and your competition.

While this is the end of the book, it doesn't have to be the end of your exploration. We have a companion website ey.com/capitalagenda that maintains supplemental material and regularly refreshes the ideas we've discussed.

Notes

1. Relative market share indexes a business's traditional market share by dividing by the share of the leading competitor. RMS for the leading competitor is calculated by dividing its share by that of the next-largest company. In each case revenues to the end customer are used.
2. The experience curve states that for every doubling of production the unit cost will decline by a fixed amount. For example, if your cost for the first 100 units was US$100 per unit and for the second 100 units (for a total of 200—a doubling) was 20% less, US$80, then your unit cost for the next 200 units (another doubling) would be 20% less still, or US$64.
3. Martin Reeves, Sandy Moose, and Thijs Venema, "BCG Classics Revisited: The Growth Share Matrix," The Boston Consulting Group, Inc., 4 June 2014.

Glossary

A
ABL: Asset-based loan. Financing secured by collateral (e.g. equipment).
Analytics: Delivery of insights through descriptive visualizations of historical trends, as well as advanced predictive and prescriptive models based on large data sets.
AP: Accounts payable.
AR: Accounts receivable.
Arbitrageur: A person simultaneously buying and selling assets, in order to take advantage of differing prices.

B
B2B: Business to business.
Brand voice: The powerful, consistent expression of a brand through words and style.

C
Capex: Capital expenditures. Funds used to acquire, upgrade, and maintain physical assets such as property, plant, and equipment.
Capital instruments: Equity securities (usually known as stock) and debt securities.
Capital markets: Financial markets in which debt and equity securities are bought and sold.
Capital structure: The mix of debt and equity used to fund a company's operations and finance its assets.
Cash conversion cycle: A measure of working capital management efficiency equal to DSO plus DIO minus DPO.

Chapter 11: The section of the United States Bankruptcy Code that provides for reorganization.

Cloud, the: Cloud computing refers to storing and accessing data, and executing programs over the internet instead of on a local network.

Corporate development: The business function or group that primarily supports inorganic growth through acquisitions, mergers, alliances, joint ventures, and partnerships.

C-suite: Senior executives, typically CEO, CFO, chief operating officer (COO), business unit leaders, and heads of functions such as supply chain, IT, and finance.

D

DBS: Danaher Business System.

DCF: Discounted cash flow. A method of valuing a project, company, or asset by calculating the present value of estimated future cash flows using an appropriate cost of capital.

DFY: Done for you.

DIO: Days inventory outstanding.

DIY: Do it yourself.

DPO: Days payable outstanding.

DSO: Days sales outstanding.

Due diligence: A comprehensive investigation undertaken by a prospective buyer to assess potential risks, including, but not limited to, those related to financial performance, commercial potential, tax, legal matters, human resources, and cybersecurity.

E

EBITDA: Earnings before interest, taxes, depreciation, and amortization.

EBITDA bridge: A decomposition of the factors causing EBITDA to change from one time period to another.

Entity priority model: In the context of a complex restructuring, a model that illustrates which stakeholders have a financial interest and which may be "out of the money."

EPS: Earnings per share.

ERP system: Enterprise resource planning system. Software that enables integrated management of core business processes.

EV/EBITDA: A valuation multiple calculated as the ratio of enterprise value to EBITDA.

F

FTE: Full-time equivalent.

G

GDP: Gross domestic product.

Glassdoor: A website www.glassdoor.com where current and former employees anonymously review companies and their management.

Google Alerts: A content change and notification service offered by Google.

Governance: The mechanisms, processes, and relationships by which corporations are controlled and directed.

H

Hurdle rate: The minimum rate that a company expects to earn when investing in a project.

Hybrid instruments: Securities with characteristics of both debt and equity (e.g., a convertible bond is a debt instrument that can be converted to equity).

I

Inorganic growth: The growth of a firm through acquisitions, mergers, alliances, joint ventures, or partnerships.

Integration playbook: A set of leading practices to guide an organization through the complexities of the acquisition process to a successful result.

Intrinsic value: The fundamental worth of a business based on the present value of its future cash flows at a point in time, which may or may not be similar to its market capitalization.

IRR: Internal rate of return.

IT: Information technology.

L

LBO: Leveraged buyout.

M

M&A: Mergers and acquisitions.

Market capitalization: For a publicly traded company, the aggregate value of its outstanding stock.

Market value: The price a willing buyer would pay for an asset.

N

NPV: Net present value.

O

OECD: Organisation for Economic Co-operation and Development.

Organic growth: The growth of a company through increased sales of existing products or new products developed internally.

Organizational silos: A mindset present when certain business units, functions, or groups within the same company do not readily share information or work together effectively.

P

Performance metrics: Quantitative and qualitative measures used to set organizational goals and assess progress.

PIR: Post-investment review.

Premortem: A decision-making technique whereby team members first anticipate the possible reasons an investment could fail. Then the terms of the project are revised to raise the odds of success.

R

R&D: Research and development.

REIT: Real estate investment trust.

Revenue synergies: The incremental revenue an acquirer and target can generate together, beyond what they would have been able to achieve individually.

RFP: Request for proposal.

ROIC: Return on invested capital.

S

Section 220: Under Delaware law, the basis for a stockholder to demand access to a company's books and records.

Secured debt instruments: Debt that is collateralized or backed by a guarantor.

SFO: Strategy, finance, and operations. The key internal stakeholder groups that make and implement complex decisions within an organization.

SG&A: Selling, general, and administrative expenses.

SOTP: Sum-of-the-parts valuation analysis. A method for estimating the total value of an enterprise by valuing its individual businesses or segments.

Supply chain: A network of organizations, people, activities, information, and other resources involved in producing and delivering products and services.

T

Terabyte: A measurement of digital capacity equal to one trillion bytes.

13-D: A Securities and Exchange Commission filing required to be submitted by anyone who acquires beneficial ownership of 5% or more of a company's equity securities.

TMA: Transition manufacturing agreement.

TSA: Transition services agreement.

TSR: Total shareholder return. A performance measure that combines share price appreciation and dividend yield.

U

Unsecured debt instruments: Any type of debt or general obligation not collateralized or protected by a guarantor.

V

Value break: In a financial restructuring, an analysis that determines the most senior creditor class that will not be paid in full, based on the estimated enterprise value of the company.

Virtual carve-out: A simulated divestment of a business as a way to understand the feasibility of a transaction and to surface possible cost-cutting opportunities.

W

WADC: Weighted average days to collect.

WAT: Weighted average terms.

Contributor Biographies

Bill Achtmeyer
EY Global Leader, EY-Parthenon, Ernst & Young LLP
Parthenon Founder
+1 617 478 4600
bill.achtmeyer@parthenon.ey.com
Bill Achtmeyer has guided Parthenon's vision since its founding in 1991. In 2014, Parthenon merged with EY, and Bill continues to lead the EY-Parthenon team in EY Transaction Advisory Services.

Bill has worked in management consulting for more than 35 years, advising CEOs on the strategic direction of their corporations.

He is a recognized authority on corporate and business unit strategy, and in mergers and acquisitions.

Subin Baral
Partner, Ernst & Young LLP
+1 212 773 1022
subin.baral@ey.com
Subin Baral has more than 10 years of experience serving life science companies in planning and executing transactions—acquisitions, carve-outs, and IPOs—from start-up through successful public company status in the United States and Australia.

He provides buy-side and sell-side support for corporate and private equity clients, especially in evaluating investment opportunities and advising on large global carve-outs.

Subin's experience spans many subsectors of the life sciences industry, including medical technology devices, pharmaceuticals, biotechnology, health care information technology, and contract manufacturing organizations.

Harsha Basnayake
EY Asia-Pacific Managing Partner
Transaction Advisory Services
+65 6309 6741
harsha.basnayake@sg.ey.com
Harsha Basnayake has more than 20 years of experience across Asia in advising clients on complex cross-border transactions, private and public sector capital decisions, and building services for EY throughout the Asia-Pacific region. His primary focus is in valuation, financial modeling, mergers and acquisitions, and restructuring. He helped to redefine EY's Transaction Advisory Services presence in the Asia-Pacific region, beginning in Singapore.

Prior to that, Harsha led Valuation and Business Modeling services in the Far East markets and was a member of EY's first Global Valuation and Business Modeling Steering Committee. He continues to be a practicing valuation professional for litigation disputes in international arbitrations and civil proceedings.

Harsha holds a number of professional affiliations and is the current Chairman of the Council of the Institute of Valuers and Appraisers of Singapore.

Sven Braun
Principal, Ernst & Young LLP
+1 415 373 2637
sven.braun@ey.com
Sven Braun works with large corporate and private equity clients to improve supply chains and operations. He focuses on freeing up cash from operations through improved working capital management, reduced costs, and increased service quality.

He is responsible for delivering client services and leads EY's digital working capital innovation group for North America. Sven has led complex engagements focused on strategy, supply chain optimization, working capital management, and transactions.

Sven has more than 15 years of experience in both industry and consulting across the globe, and he has worked across a broad spectrum of sectors, including high tech, IT, automotive, pharmaceuticals, and industrial goods.

K.C. Brechnitz
EY Global Head, Debt Capital Markets Advisory
Senior Managing Director, Ernst & Young Capital
Advisors, LLC
+1 704 335 4211
kc.brechnitz@ey.com
K.C. Brechnitz leads the organization's debt capital markets efforts globally. He provides independent advice on raising and restructuring capital.

K.C. has 20 years of experience in debt capital markets, including leveraged finance, high-yield capital markets, restructuring advisory, and loan syndications. His track record includes extensive work in PE-sponsored leveraged buyouts and complex acquisition financings. His sector experience is in gaming, consumer and retail, business services, and general industrial.

Since starting the Debt Capital Markets Advisory practice within Ernst & Young Capital Advisors, LLC in 2010, K.C. has personally worked on more than US$30 billion in capital transactions.

Daniel Burkly
Senior Manager, Ernst & Young LLP
+1 312 879 2575
daniel.burkly@ey.com
Daniel Burkly serves as a transaction leader for several large multinationals, consulting on strategy, valuation, due diligence, and integration.

Dan applies his technical background in corporate finance and valuation to advise clients on the financial implications of their strategic decisions. He has performed thousands of financial analyses and valuations of businesses, equity interests, debt instruments, and various assets and liabilities for transaction planning, corporate planning, tax planning and reporting, and financial reporting purposes.

Dan's clients include Fortune 500 companies in life sciences, diversified industrial products, and consumer products industries.

He has spoken and written on corporate finance topics, including share repurchases and valuation techniques. He is a Chartered Financial Analyst charter holder and has served as a grader for CFA Level III exams.

William Casey
EY Americas Vice Chair, Transaction Advisory Services
Ernst & Young, LLP
+1 212 773 0058
william.casey@ey.com

William Casey has 35 years of experience advising clients on capital strategy, mergers and acquisitions, spinoffs, IPOs, and securities offerings. As EY's TAS leader in the Americas and in prior roles as its Deputy Leader and Chief Operating Officer, he has overseen a doubling of the practice, to nearly 5,000 professionals in the United States, Canada, Mexico, and Central and South America.

William has led some of EY's largest client engagements in industries including automotive, beverages, telecommunications, fintech, and professional services. He has advised on cross-border transactions for multinational corporations and leading private equity firms in both the US and Latin America.

William is a Certified Public Accountant, fluent in English, Spanish, and Portuguese, and a competitive triathlete.

Glenn Engler
EY Americas Digital Strategy Leader, EY-Parthenon,
Ernst & Young LLP
+1 617 478 7095
glenn.engler@parthenon.ey.com

Glenn Engler focuses primarily on growth strategy, marketing strategy, brand development, and new business innovation in several industries, including technology, media, telecommunications, retail, and automotive. In addition, Glenn leads the digital practices for EY-Parthenon globally, and leads digital strategy for Transaction Advisory Services in the Americas.

Prior to joining EY-Parthenon, Glenn spent more than 25 years in the strategy consulting, marketing communications, digital marketing, customer relationship management, and social media areas.

Donald Featherstone
EY EMEIA Restructuring Leader
+44 (0) 207 951 9554
dfeatherstone@uk.ey.com
Donald Featherstone leads EY's EMEIA Restructuring services. He has more than 25 years of experience in corporate turnarounds, large-scale financial restructurings, interim management, and board mandates. He has been appointed as an interim executive in numerous engagements across a variety of industries.

Don has assisted public and private companies with complex capital structure reshaping, stakeholder negotiations, and the execution of operational turnaround programs. He has worked extensively on cross-border restructuring engagements in the European Union and United States, and in emerging markets in South America, the Middle East, and Africa.

Shyam Gidumal
Activist Advisory Leader
Northeast Region Retail & Consumer Products Leader,
Ernst & Young LLP
+1 212 773 3414
shyam.gidumal@ey.com
Shyam Gidumal leads EY's work around activist investors.

Over the past 30 years, Shyam has been a principal investor, buy-side and sell-side advisor, board member, strategic/operational consultant, chief restructuring officer, and president and CEO across multiple large-cap and mid-cap companies. Prior to joining EY, Shyam was a partner and Member of the Board of the Boston Consulting Group, a senior managing director of AlixPartners, founder of Strategic Turnarounds & Investment Corp., and a General Partner with Stonington Partners.

Shyam has worked extensively in France, Germany, Greece, Hong Kong, India, Japan, Singapore, and the UK.

242

Jeffrey R. Greene
Leader, Corporate Development Leadership Network
+1 917 443 5049
jeffrey.greene@ey.com
Jeffrey R. Greene leads EY's Corporate Development Leadership Network—an invitation-only, permanent roundtable of the heads of M&A, strategy, and inorganic growth for 40 of the largest companies in North America. His previous roles include Global Vice Chair-Corporate Finance and EY Global Transactions Leader for the Life Sciences Sector.

With more than three decades of transaction experience, he counsels senior executives on the corporate finance implications of their strategic and operating decisions. Jeff provides valuation advice in divestments, acquisitions, financings, and restructurings. He is also a recognized expert witness in federal, district, bankruptcy, and tax courts on valuation, fairness, and solvency matters.

Jeff has spoken, written, and been quoted on life sciences industry developments, as well as the Capital Agenda, including M&A, portfolio management, valuation, solvency, and performance measurement.

Paul Hammes
EY Global Divestiture Advisory Services Leader
EY Global Transaction Diligence Leader
+1 312 879 3741
paul.hammes@ey.com
Paul Hammes serves private equity and corporate clients on the buy and sell sides. For the past 12 years he has provided dedicated divestment advice to Fortune 100, 500, and 1000 companies, as well as to numerous privately held and PE-backed companies.

Paul's industry experience includes more than 300 transactions across manufacturing, chemicals, plastics, wholesale/distribution, consumer products, trucking, education, aerospace and defense, and life sciences.

Paul is a certified public accountant with more than 28 years of business experience.

Julie Hood
EY Global Deputy Vice Chair, Transaction Advisory
Services
EY Global Limited
+ 44 (0) 20 7980 0327
julie.hood@uk.ey.com
Julie Hood, with her team across 90 countries, works to
solve the most pressing business challenges, helping com-
panies better manage their capital across five connected solutions of strategy, corporate finance, buying and integrating, selling and separating, and reshaping results.

In her time at EY, Julie has advised clients across a broad range of industries,
establishing a deep level of operational transactional understanding of organizations
in Asia, Europe, and the Americas. Before EY, Julie worked in the higher education
sector and ran her own design consulting and construction business.

Steve Krouskos
EY Global Vice Chair, Transaction Advisory Services
EY Global Limited
+44 (0) 20 7980 0189
steve.krouskos@uk.ey.com
Steve Krouskos has more than 25 years of experience
in M&A, advising corporate and private equity clients on
multibillion-dollar, cross-border transactions.
Steve chairs the TAS Global Executive, and is a member of the EY Global Board.
He is responsible for driving growth and investment priorities for Transaction
Advisory Services and delivering exceptional client service around the world.

He played a pivotal role in the successful EY-Parthenon combination. He is also
the senior advisory partner to several global EY accounts.

Steve has served clients across a wide range of industries spanning consumer
products and retail, industrial products, life sciences, transportation and logistics,
technology, communications, professional services, and franchising.

Erica Lawee
EY Global Development Leader, Transaction Tax
+44 (0) 20 7980 0430
erica.lawee@uk.ey.com
Erica Lawee works to develop and implement a cohesive growth strategy for the global Transaction Tax practices. She also focuses on private equity markets, working closely with EY's PE tax leadership and clients to formulate and execute strategy and enable growth in PE accounts.

Erica oversees the global coordination of EY's tax director conferences for the fund sector.

Erica advises on both buy-side and sell-side tax due diligence, as well as on tax-efficient holding and financing structures for cross-border M&A transactions.

Steve Payne
EY Americas Deputy Vice Chair, Transaction Advisory Services
EY Global Leader, Operational Transaction Services
+1 212 773 0562
steve.payne@ey.com
Steve Payne has held several roles in his nine years at EY, including Americas Capital Transformation Leader, Northeast TAS Regional Leader, and Americas Working Capital Leader.

At EY and throughout his career, Steve has led many large global working capital improvement programs for private equity houses and Fortune 50 clients, including large global pharmaceutical companies.

Prior to joining EY, Steve was the President of REL Consultancy, a division of the Hackett Group, a public consulting firm. Steve has held positions at HarperCollins and ML Aviation.

Tony Qui
EY Global Innovation and Digital Leader, Transaction Advisory Services
+44 (0) 20 7951 5820
tqui@uk.ey.com
Tony Qui heads EY teams comprising more than 1,500 transaction professionals. His experience spans a wide range of sectors, including consumer products, energy, pharmaceuticals, telecoms, media, oil and gas, mining, and financial services.

Tony has led more than 200 transactions involving information technology due diligence, digital strategy, IT cost-reduction assessments, buy-side, vendor, carve-outs, contract exits, postmerger integration, and operational restructuring. He has more than 15 years of experience in leading major change programs.

Brian Salsberg
EY Americas M&A Integration Leader
EY Global Buy and Integrate Leader
+1 212 773 3462
brian.salsberg@ey.com
Brian Salsberg is responsible for leading and enhancing EY's capabilities and intellectual capital around mergers, acquisitions, and joint venture integration.

He spent 13 years at McKinsey & Company, where he led dozens of strategy-, growth-, and transaction-related engagements as part of the New York, Tokyo, and Singapore offices.

Brian was previously Senior Vice President of Global Strategy at Avon Products, Inc., where he reported to the CEO and was a member of the Executive Committee. His leadership responsibilities included corporate and business development, as well as global digital.

Brian began his career as a transaction attorney at a top five global M&A law firm, Cravath, Swaine & Moore.

Sharath Sharma

EY Americas Capital Transformation Leader, Ernst & Young LLP

+1 212 773 6190

sharath.sharma@ey.com

Sharath Sharma has served as a journey partner to CEOs and CFOs on many significant transactions. He advises his clients on strategy and operations matters and helps them to manage acquisitions, divestments, and joint ventures throughout the transaction life cycle.

He focuses on providing desired deal outcomes. His experience in supply chain strategy, enterprise cost reduction, organization design, and governance enables him to serve as a trusted advisor to executives in the strategy, finance, and operations domains.

Sharath has worked in the industrial products, life sciences, and consumer products sectors. He has served client needs in Mexico, Canada, Brazil, Spain, the United Kingdom, Germany, India, China, and Singapore.

John Trustman

Executive Director, EY-Parthenon, Ernst & Young LLP

+1 617 478 4399

john.trustman@parthenon.ey.com

John Trustman leads the development and deployment of EY's proprietary framework, the Full Potential Paradigm, within the EY-Parthenon strategy team.

John's 40-year career as a strategy consultant, executive, and entrepreneur spans numerous industries, with a concentration in health care, financial services, and technology.

John holds patents in a range of disciplines from brainwave analysis and movement disorder diagnosis to natural language processing and large-scale transaction processing.

Aayush Tulsyan
Senior Manager, Ernst & Young LLP
+1 312 879 2965
aayush.tulsyan@ey.com

Aayush Tulsyan's transaction work focuses on sell-side due diligence, operational separation, and post-close stabilization. He has advised on multiple complex cross-border transactions across Europe, Asia, and South America.

Aayush has experience in finance process improvement, enterprise cost reduction, operating model design, and driver-based planning projects in the life sciences, aerospace and defense, consumer products, and heavy equipment manufacturing sectors.

Giri Varadarajan
Accounts and Pursuits Leader, Transaction Advisory Services, Ernst & Young LLP
+1 312 879 3259
giri.varadarajan@ey.com

Giri Varadarajan, has over the past 15 years, advised C-suite executives and private equity clients in driving operating margin and capital efficiency improvements. He helps multinational firms in consumer goods, health care, industrial products, and process industries take advantage of strategic and operational opportunities.

His significant transactions work focuses on complex integrations and carve-outs. Giri's experience also includes developing and supporting the implementation of value-creation programs focused on enterprise cost reduction, supply-chain transformations, outsourcing/offshoring, pricing, and portfolio optimization.

He has led global engagements with clients in Mexico, Canada, Brazil, the United Kingdom, Germany, Italy, Romania, Hungary, India, China, and Australia.

Bridget Walsh
EY Global Transaction Tax Leader, EY Global Limited
+44 (0) 20 7951 4176
bwalsh@uk.ey.com
Bridget Walsh has almost 20 years of experience in tax, many of which have been spent advising private equity houses, other fund investors, and corporations on tax aspects of acquisitions and divestments.

Bridget has successfully held a number of senior leadership roles in the EY UK&I region, including Head of Private Equity, China Trade Route Leader, and Head of Transaction Tax. She is also the lead relationship partner for some of the organization's largest PE fund clients.

Bridget has significant experience in working with corporations, banks, and PE houses to structure transactions and manage the tax aspects of transactions, including funding, valuation, modeling, and sale and purchase review.

Andrew Wollaston
EY Global Restructuring Advisory Leader
EY Global Private Equity Leader
+44 (0) 20 7951 9944
awollaston@uk.ey.com
Andrew Wollaston has more than 25 years of experience in advising stakeholders of underperforming businesses and of assisting in the recovery of ailing companies. He has led a wide variety of assignments in most industry sectors and geographies.

Andrew now principally executes financial advisor mandates for corporations and stakeholders in debt restructurings and refinancings. He also takes on chief restructuring officer roles, and has advised on and helped to implement operational turnarounds and distressed M&A services.

Jeff Wray
Consumer Products Leader, EY-Parthenon, Ernst & Young LLP
+1 215 448 4099
jeff.wray@ey.com
Jeff Wray has more than 20 years of experience in developing strategy and driving large-scale operational change, primarily in consumer products categories.

His deal track record includes small-scale growth, corporate venture capital, large-scale divestments, and M&A.

Jeff has worked with businesses in Asia, the Middle East, North America, and Latin America.

About EY

EY is a global leader in assurance, tax, transaction, and advisory services. The insights and quality services we deliver help build trust and confidence in the capital markets and in economies the world over. We develop outstanding leaders who team to deliver on our promises to all of our stakeholders. In so doing, we play a critical role in building a better working world for our people, for our clients, and for our communities.

EY refers to the global organization, and may refer to one or more, of the member firms of Ernst & Young Global Limited, each of which is a separate legal entity. Ernst & Young Global Limited, a UK company limited by guarantee, does not provide services to clients. For more information about our organization, please visit ey.com.

About EY's Transaction Advisory Services

How you manage your Capital Agenda today will define your competitive position tomorrow. We work with clients to create social and economic value by helping them make better, more informed decisions about strategically managing capital and transactions in fast-changing markets. Whether you're preserving, optimizing, raising, or investing capital, EY's Transaction Advisory Services combine a set of skills, insight, and experience to deliver focused advice. We can help you drive competitive advantage and increased returns through improved decisions across all aspects of your Capital Agenda.

ey.com/capitalagenda

This material has been prepared for general informational purposes only and is not intended to be relied upon as accounting, tax or other professional advice. Please refer to your advisors for specific advice.

The views of the third parties set out in this publication are not necessarily the views of the global EY organization or its member firms. Moreover, they should be seen in the context of the time they were made.

Index